LOST ICONS

LOST ICONS

Reflections on Cultural Bereavement

ROWAN WILLIAMS

MOREHOUSE PUBLISHING
A Continuum imprint
HARRISBURG • LONDON • NEW YORK

Morehouse Publishing

A *Continuum imprint*

4775 Linglestown Road
Harrisburg, PA 17112
USA

First published 2000
Reprinted 2000, 2001, 2002 (twice)

ISBN 0–8192–1948–7

*In memory of Murray Cox
and Gillian Rose*

Contents

Preface

There have been times when I thought this book might more honestly have been presented as a sort of journal of the 1990s. It has been several years in the making, and has been constantly reshaped as the decade unfolded (including a change of government in Britain and a war or two elsewhere). But the reflections here set down still seemed to circle around a few fundamental themes, and to make something a little like a connected argument; so it remains in the shape of an essay. I hope, though, that its readers will try to discern behind the surface a continuing story of reaction to the strange decade that has closed the twentieth century, a decade that has given us plenty to worry about, economically, internationally and culturally; most worrying, perhaps, because of our awkwardness in confronting the fact that certain styles of human self-understanding, styles that might conduce to a sense of irony or humility or trustfulness or solidarity, are fast becoming unavailable. This book attempts to identify some of these and to interpret and even defend them before they are quite forgotten. It does so from the point of view of a Christian priest; but I hope that most of what is written here will be accessible to those who do not share the theological position from which I begin.

The conversations that have helped to form this book have been with many people over many more years than it has taken (even) to write it. I must express my debt to my wife Jane; to Val Martin and my colleagues in the Church in Wales Division for Social Responsibility; to Tim Jenkins, Sara Maitland, John and Alison Milbank, Catherine Pickstock, Paul Rahe and Graham Ward. The dedication of the book inadequately marks two especially deep influences, personal, spiritual and intellectual. I miss them grievously and give thanks for them.

ROWAN WILLIAMS
Newport, July 1999

Introduction

The word 'icon' has come down in the world. It is probably more familiar as a term of art in the world of communication technology than as the designation of a sacred image; perhaps for most people its commonest use is to designate a particular kind of public figure. 'Icons' appear on computer screens or on television screens. They classify instructions for managing a machine or they mark the fashionable significance of a singer, model, actor or sporting hero. The late Princess Diana was regularly described as an 'icon'; Madonna and the Spice Girls likewise (interestingly, it seems to be a word applied more easily to women than to men in our culture, even in fashionable talk about 'gay icons'). An icon is apparently in this context something like a classic statement of a particular kind of life, a particular kind of *style*. This may not necessarily be a life or a style simply presented as something to *aspire* to, an ideal; 'iconic' status means something more like becoming part of the code of a community, becoming in some way an image that binds people together, provides a common point of reference and a common touchstone of acceptability. A mediaeval commentator might have said that it was a shared source of 'delight' ... Its meaning belongs in the complex realm of public presentation, the marketing of personalities. It defines possibilities for a cultural group; it doesn't need a reference in some represented or evoked reality beyond itself, because its power and substance lie in its capacity to focus the desires of a public or a constituency. It 'refers' to these desires, it represents imagined futures; in itself, it needs no relation to a hinterland of meaning. It aims at an authoritative, self-contained presence – an *obviousness* in its structure and conventions.

But there are other meanings to be retrieved or suggested. The traditional icon of the Eastern Christian world is never meant to be a reproduction of the realities you see around you; it is not even meant to show what these realities will ever look like. It shows some part of this world – a scene from history, from the Bible, a particular person or group of persons – within a structure that puts them in a distinctive light. What is shown is their significance against the background of a source of illumination independent of them. This is, incidentally, illustrated graphically by the convention in iconography of building up the colours on a gold base: from this the rest of the representation 'emerges'. The point of the icon is to give us a window into an alien frame of reference that is at the same time the structure that will make definitive sense of the world we inhabit. It is sometimes described as a channel for the 'energies' of that other frame of reference to be transmitted to the viewer.

Something of this is what I want to explore here. Human cultures, up to the dawn of modernity, have generally worked with verbal and moral 'icons' – patterns of reading and understanding human behaviour and relationship that don't simply arise from what any particular group happens to find helpful or interesting, but that are supposed to represent some of the basic constraints on what human beings can reasonably do and say together if they are going to remain within a recognisably human conversation. It is a cliché and an unhelpful one to observe that these structures have not been universally the same. The point is that they have been there at all. The sort of thing I mean would include, for example: language about kinship; ritual marking of death and a set of conventions about what to do with human corpses; the ritualisation of eating; the regulation of sexual activity; the assumption that there are appropriately different expectations of human beings at different stages in their lives, and various ways of codifying these; the making of promises; the recitations of a common history. All have in common the presupposition that we cannot choose just any course of action in respect of our human and non-human environment and still expect to 'make sense' – that is, to be part of a serious human conversation in which our actions can be evaluated and thought through and drawn into some sort of rough coherence, by ourselves and by other speakers. These are not moral ideals or demands, in the sense of being things required by authority for the sake of a granting of approval; they are a bit more basic, to do with the conditions of common life and language. They are, in what is now a well-known phrase, the points or levels in human talking 'where our spade is turned'. Where such things obtain, people do not know how to *belong* with each other and with their environment in the absence of these – what should we call them? Not conventions, as that implies a certain contingency or arbitrariness in them, nor ideals, as they are not goals to be pursued; hence my choice of 'icons', structures for seeing and connecting in the light of something other than our decisions, individual or corporate.

Modernity has been suspicious of all this, assuming that the reasoning mind can sort out a sensible common agenda for human beings, a process in which these 'iconic' structures will either prove their rational usefulness or turn out to be, indeed, arbitrary and therefore deserve to be discarded. The result – a banal enough observation, this – has been a prolonged and highly complicated story in which 'modern' society, mostly North European and North Atlantic, has tried to disentangle structures that have served limited and oppressive interests, yet have been defended and justified as 'natural', from those that have some claim to be intrinsic to human welfare and sense. The very recognition of the former has made it harder to identify the latter: suspicion becomes endemic. Current confusion over the family or gender roles or 'sexual preference', over religion and secularity, over race, sovereignty, language and economics and many other things suggests that no consensus is going to appear in a hurry, whatever pressures there are to identify 'values' we hold in common.

So this short essay does not set out to offer any theories about the precise content of a plausible list of iconic structures. More modestly, it looks at a limited number of areas in which some kinds of discourse seem to be getting more and more laboured, more and more inaccessible to our culture; and it asks whether the consequences of the loss of these icons might not imperil so deeply the possibilities of corporate sense-making (and so of just social order) as to suggest that here we might find a few pointers to where

4

spades are turned. It will be clear that the practical concerns behind this book have a lot to do with the education of our children. The first chapter presses the question of whether we now have any confidence about what we mean by 'childhood' in our culture; because if we haven't, there is no chance at all of our having a coherent idea of what education might be. But there is a further suggestion, that we won't make sense of childhood unless we have an idea of what we understand by *choice*; and the background question is, What happens to our sense of the human when it is divorced from a grasp of the self as something realised *in time*? The 'iconic' issue here is how far a picture of the human as constructing identities in would-be independence of the temporal flow can serve as a structure for human sense.

In fact, this issue, in one way or another, will be around throughout these pages. The second chapter looks at the erosion of those mechanisms in society that control or limit rivalry – particularly those that have little to do with conscious choice or policy. To recognise that the choices of the individual will cannot demand instant and unconditional fulfilment in the material and inhabited world we in fact live in is to acknowledge the necessity of spending time in the management of conflicts of interest or desire. But the readiness to spend time in this way already presupposes certain bonds, certain convergences of interest. Paradoxically, to be able to 'negotiate' differences (rather than trying to resolve them by the contest of violence) entails an assumption that differences can be *thought*, not just thrown against each other; that the present conversation takes for granted a common world and that the interests of its inhabitants can never be intelligibly

considered except by thinking of relations and interdependence, even if only at a very formal level. But to arrive
at this understanding involves the recognition that the self
itself is learned or evolved, not a given, fixed system of
needs and desires. And this leads on in turn to a reflection
in the third chapter on the phenomenon of *remorse*, in
which we come to terms with the unwelcome fact of our
presence in other people's histories, a presence we can't
control. There is that of us, it seems, which lives outside
what we think of as ourselves.

Following through the implication of this leads to the
further acknowledgement that my loss and the loss of other
subjects (that is, other feeling and thinking entities) are
not two distinct matters: my life-in-the-other, theirs in me,
means that it is possible to discover a kind of 'mourning'
that does justice not simply to any individual's privation or
pain but to the shared nature of human grief. Again
paradoxically, comedy as well as tragedy carries that recognition; both are potentially painful to the extent that they
constantly undermine self-contained and controlled
models of the self. And in the final section of these reflections, the conclusion is drawn out that what is common to
all the imaginative crises and deprivations discussed is the
loss of the language of the *soul*.

The last chapter attempts the ambitious and indeed
thankless task of defining what this might mean.
Something other than arguing about the presence or
absence of a supposedly non-material 'element' in the
human constitution is involved, and this discussion takes
it for granted that the post-Freudian insistence that the self
is not a *given* form of inner unity has to be given due
weight. One recent writer has spoken of the self as what

emerges in the process of 'defining conflicts' – that is, conflicts that provoke sufficient interrogation to generate a new way of speaking, of articulating a position. In a culture that tries hard to minimise certain sorts of conflict or contradiction – either by a mythology of the goodness and givenness of an inner self or by the (equally mythological) picture of the agent as simply enacting a chaos of timeless desires – a vital language of selfhood wastes away. But in using the word 'soul' as well as 'self', in treating the latter as very nearly a synonym for the former, I have deliberately trailed a coat. 'Soul' is – at least – a religious style of talking about selfhood; and the issue finally raised here is whether a wholly secular language for the self can resist the trivialisations and reductions outlined in the book as a whole. This is dangerous territory. It is religious language that has borne most of the responsibility for keeping alive the story of a substantial soul that can live apart from the body and its history, and it may seem an odd ally to turn to in order to challenge just that model. But, if for the moment we keep our distance from what might be properly called religious doctrine, and ask about the nature of the religious self as articulated in some styles of religious culture, mainly but not exclusively Christian, I hope that the relevance of these styles to our present cultural bereavement may emerge as worth discussing. It is certainly interesting that psychoanalytic theory continues to engage in a cautious and complicated pavane with the language of the Christian tradition in seeking to make sense of how the self is formed in response not simply to the contingent other, but to an Other which may be necessarily fictive and empty – or necessarily not, depending on a good many variable and involved factors.

So this is an essay about the erosions of selfhood in North Atlantic modernity; and also, therefore, about the accompanying erosion of certain ways of imagining *time*. It will emerge, I think, how these issues are bound up together. Wilfully standing back from the different kinds of questions about how meaning relates to a history of *production*,[1] the common feature in many of the areas discussed here, leaves us with one or another form of the given and absolute self, the self that stands outside language and interchange. Now to use a term like 'production' invites the suspicion of Marxist influence; but in fact one of the really substantive *philosophical* insights of Marxism was to focus attention on the ways in which meaning is bound up with the processes by which we engage and transform a material environment. It also alerts us to the fact that cultural questions can't be separated ultimately from questions about power – about who has the freedom for what kinds of transformation of an environment. Chatter of a certain kind about freedom of choice needs chastening by reflection on who is being served by particular models of freedom, since there is no possibility of talking usefully about freedom without looking at the way power is distributed in actual societies.

These will be issues in the background rather than the foreground of what follows; but it is important to note in advance that these broader questions of political discernment press in very insistently when we speak seriously about cultural change and cultural deprivation. Part of the frustration of our contemporary position is that

---

[1] The significance of production as an issue affecting what we say of ourselves is given prominence in Nicholas Boyle's brilliant collection of essays on our current crises, *Who Are We Now? Christian Humanism and the Global Market from Hegel to Heaney* (Edinburgh, 1998).

political language becomes increasingly dominated by the marketing of slogans, sound bites, and the calculation of short-term advantage, in a way that effectively removes politics from considerations about the transformation of human culture; while a fair amount of what passes for cultural studies relies on fundamentally anti-political accounts of desire and imagination. This book will not bridge that gap, but it is at least an attempt to read the gap as a wound, which neither conventional right nor conventional left are currently doing much to recognise or repair. Indeed, the job is *not* to 'mend' this or other breaches so much as to suggest how the raw edges can awaken us to questions about our humanity which even the most mature kinds of political and cultural discourse handle only with difficulty.

And the last introductory word, which may already have been hinted at, is that this is a book attempting to articulate *anger* – not anger only, and not necessarily an anger that requires more and more insistent and explicit statement, but anger nonetheless, at a recent history of public corruption and barbarity compounded by apathy and narcissism in our imaginative world. Fiona MacCarthy's 1994 biography of William Morris, one of the most solid and resourceful books of the decade to deal with the politics of culture and the culture of politics, concludes its introduction by evoking Morris's likely reaction to the prevailing ethos of the 1980s and 1990s.

> Electronic addiction? Drug culture? Inner city planning? Bottom line banking? Political correctness? Post-Modernist architecture? ... Sound bites? Opinion polls? Chat shows? Designer clothes? Executive phones? Pulp literature? Video porn? Corporate sponsorship? Market-orientated society?

'Damn'd pigs! Damn'd fools!' You can hear Morris expostulate, robust, fidgety, tremendous ... [2]

We seem to have no contemporary Morris; but it may still be possible to wake an echo of that imagined expostulation.

[2] Fiona MacCarthy, *William Morris. A Life for Our Times* (London, 1994), p. xix.

1

Childhood and Choice

A few years ago, the excellent education supplement of the *Guardian* carried a series of articles under the general heading of 'Education 2000'. The writers were fairly representative of educational and political orthodoxies; much emphasis was laid upon training, skills, socialisation, from contributors of the left and the right alike. The week after the series ended, there was a letter from someone who had long been engaged in some less orthodox experiments in private education; it pointed out rather acidly that not a single article in the series appeared to have contained the words 'childhood' or 'play'.

This is a heavy indictment; an accurate one, unfortunately, as far as this (in many ways admirable) series was concerned, and so a pretty accurate measure of the orthodoxies represented. What it speaks of is a profound *impatience*. Childhood, after all, is a period we've come to think of as 'latency', the time before certain determinations and decisions have to be made. But to manage such a period requires a certain confidence that the society we inhabit has the resources to carry passengers, a confidence that we know how to live alongside people whose participation in our social forms is not like ours. It is not that the child doesn't have a share in society; but, on the whole, developed and not-so-developed cultures alike have granted that the child does not have the same kind of negotiating role in society as the adult. Hence, of course, the prevalence of rituals of transition – putting on the *toga virilis*, adolescent circumcision, bar-mitzvah ... The child is brought out of a latent or free-floating state to become a social agent like you and me. But this implies that we as adult social agents are obliged to bear with what goes before, with the indeterminacies of childhood. A society with clearly marked transitional rituals is committed to *guaranteeing* the integrity of such a period; and a society for which the education of children is essentially about pressing the child into adult or pseudo-adult roles as fast as possible, is one that has lost patience with that kind of commitment.

A lot could be said about the prolonged 'latency' of the human young. It is not only a function of the sheer biological vulnerability of human infants, so much more protracted than in other species; it also has to do with the fact (connected with, but not simply reducible to, biology) that humans perceive themselves, form their attitudes to their bodies and to other bodies, as users of *language*. The acquiring and refining of language is a long and complex process, never moving at precisely the same rate in different subjects. And part of that process, as every parent and teacher is (at some level) aware, is play; because to learn language is to discover, by trial and error, what I can seriously be committed to when I open my mouth, what I'm ready to answer for. This is something I cannot begin to do with intelligence or confidence unless I am allowed to make utterances that I *don't* have to answer for. We do not treat children as adult speakers whom we expect to take straightforward responsibility for what they say according to recognisable conventions: we accept that there is a sphere of legitimately irresponsible talking, of fantasy and uninhibited role-playing, language without commitments beyond the particular game being played. Without such an acceptance, the learning of language is paralysed by the fear of making mistakes – not just mistakes in grammar or diction or whatever, but the disastrous fate of having game taken as reality, being *bound* by things thoughtlessly or ignorantly said. We are familiar, from fiction and autobiography, with the trauma that can be suffered by a child whose fantasy is taken for distorted or intended fact, whose imagination is interpreted as lying, by a hostile, stupid or tyrannous adult. And there is a sharp little tale ('The Looking-Glass Boy') by that surprising Edwardian children's writer, E. M. Nesbit, which turns on the fate of a boy who himself does not appreciate the difference between fantasy and lying; as a result of the kind of morally robust magical intervention Nesbit enjoyed providing, he has to experience as reality the fantasies he concocts – that is, he has to take responsibility for what he says. He thus learns, if in a somewhat drastic way, a lesson about adult discourse and indeed about the *social* or at least interpersonal dimension of speech. The morality of this story is crude, but it illustrates neatly the point being made – the difference between talking we can be expected to be answerable for and other kinds of talking.

Children growing into mature speakers will naturally want to try out projects and identities. Adults overhearing children fantasising (the stories a child tells herself in bed, a game in the corner of a room or a schoolyard) may be shocked at times as well as amused: the uncensored tribal mythologies of schoolchildren as collected by the Opies in their wonderful books, are shot through with fantasies of terror and violence and half-understood sexual threats. Alison Lurie observes of playground rhymes that 'everything we might want to protect boys and girls from is already in these verses'; and in her novel, *Foreign Affairs*, the central character, Vinnie Miner (a scholar of children's literature), is dismayed and disillusioned when her field research on children's rhymes and games uncovers what are to her obscene, cheap and disgusting imaginings.[1] But – without wanting to deny that children's language and imagination can genuinely be corrupted and cheapened – we have to remember the multitude of roles and vocabularies that every child uses. If we allow that there is a proper and protected space for children to be 'irresponsible' speakers, we must budget for the fact that their uncommitted speech will not be uniformly nice, docile or harmonious – understanding that the freedom to try out roles and images and words that are not 'nice' is a rather significant part of learning speech. In other words, latency should not be muddled up with *adult* fantasies of innocence.

If children's fantasies can be anarchic and amoral, or, at least, at an angle to our constructions of plausibility and rightness, it should not surprise us if the children's literature that seems to have staying power includes texts that sit light to realism or moral tidiness or both. It will seem

[1] Alison Lurie, *Foreign Affairs* (London, 1985), pp. 113–16; on playground rhymes in general, *Not in Front of the Grown-Ups: Subversive Children's Literature* (London, 1990), chapter 16 ('Everything we might want ...', p. 215).

strange, perhaps, to bracket together two such wildly different children's writers as Enid Blyton and Roald Dahl; but they have this at least in common, that they are both abidingly popular, to a degree that can be baffling to sensitive adult observers, and this despite the weight of adult disapproval, from parents, teachers and librarians. Blyton is castigated for her flatness of style, for class prejudice, stereotypical characters and speech forms, and lazy plotting; Dahl for his vulgarity, collusion with violence, sexual stereotyping, racism and cynicism. To the adult reader – in practice, the long-suffering adult reader-aloud – these charges are beyond dispute; and they are capable of uniting the orthodox of left and right in a most striking way. But what both writers do (with, I suspect, rather different levels of self-awareness) is precisely to indulge 'irresponsible talking', to inhabit the child's indeterminate world with hardly a hint of apology. Fantasy is given free rein, in a world from which 'ordinary' adult agents are largely absent. Dahl presents us with monstrous or subhuman adults, tyrants and fools, varied with rather ineffectual, if benign, elders. Blyton's still phenomenally popular 'Famous Five' books are to the adult no more than interminable and wellnigh indistinguishable variations on a single plot. The children, separated completely from their parents, engage in and solve some kind of 'mystery', usually in a mildly exotic setting (island, castle, moorland, circus). To the young reader, they are very much about the freedom to try out a sort of adult identity: to be in control of an environment where adult power and presence is not visible, *and* where the prosaic externals of the 'normal' environment in which adult power operates are also forgotten or suspended. It is because this is a non-standard environment, a holiday in unreal surroundings, with the children living unsupervised (and eating the 1950s equivalent of junk food a lot of the time) that it is possible to imagine new and unconstrained identities. This is not a world in which the ordinary sequence of acts and consequences operates at all strongly, and so it becomes possible to 'speak without commitment', to test possible courses of action without anxiety, to try on clothes.

A recent and highly provocative study of children's fantasy by John Goldthwaite argues with passion that: 'To pretend that children's books are the playground of the imagination, with no intrinsic pedagogic content and no accountability to reality, is to deny the very nature of the reading experience in childhood';[2] on this basis, a number of classics in the canon (including *Alice* and the Narnia books of C. S. Lewis) are severely castigated for erroneous teaching about the world. Either, like *Alice*, they lack – or even subvert – coherent moral purpose,[3] or, like Narnia, they inculcate false and (surprisingly) blasphemous views of the world. In the latter case, fantasy becomes a malign substitute for the real world, a place to work out grievances against the world God has actually made, rather than a space for learning how the real world may properly and faithfully be negotiated.[4] There is some point to this thesis, though I find its characterisation of a good many

[2] John Goldthwaite, *The Natural History of Make-Believe. A Guide to the Principal Works of Britain, Europe and America* (Oxford/New York, 1996), p. 195.

[3] Ibid. chapter 3; pp. 164ff. on 'the absence of *agape*' ['love' as in Paul's first Epistle to the Corinthians].

[4] Ibid. pp. 220–44, esp. 242 ('This is what you do when your God asks things of you that are unthinkable; you create another world where you can sneak in your complaints under the guise of make-believe').

writers, not only Carroll and Lewis, eccentric and overdrawn. What matters is indeed where we end up, what moral suppleness and insight have been won in the course of the story; and in such a light it is hard to rule wholly out of court the 'parallel world' style of fantasy, as exemplified in Lewis and his precursors and imitators. (It is equally hard, I'd say, to rule out the kind of anarchic and parodic fantasy found at its darkest in *Alice* and at what Goldthwaite terms its most 'frivolous' in Jim Henson's triumphantly surreal adaptations of children's classics for his Muppets; Goldthwaite, sadly, doesn't at all approve of these resourceful and ironic transformations.[5]) The salient question is whether and how we are returned to our own setting, and how, in the interim, we have learned to 'read' it. Lewis sails very near the wind, admittedly, in including a final Narnian episode dealing, a little ambitiously, with the end of the space-time universe: the sequence does indeed seem to end in a decisive escape from the choices and tensions of the temporal order. And the way in which 'Narnian' lessons are put into practice in our world can indeed look lame at best and at worst just as silly and offensive as Goldthwaite argues. Yet the lessons themselves can often stand; the problem is less, I think, with Lewis's method than with his unmistakeable clumsiness in handling a good many aspects of the contemporary world in plausible fictional terms.[6]

---

[5] Ibid. p. 195: 'it teaches frivolity' is his judgement on the Muppet Workshop.

[6] Lewis's best effort, *That Hideous Strength*, must be set against this negative assessment; but, despite its considerable achievement in savage satire of a realistic kind, it is strongest when dealing with the invasion of the contemporary by the mythical. Goldthwaite's annihilating hostility to Lewis overall ignores Lewis's extraordinary ability, at his very best, both to relativise his own prejudices and to uncover moral self-deception at every level.

The 'alternative world' vein has been mined almost to exhaustion in the past few decades, though new publications continually recycle its themes. Like Blyton's books, these fantasies are often flawed by stereotypes of class, race and sex, and present, to adult eyes, anything but a morally rounded universe. But the basic premise, that children may find themselves transported to a magical or mythological level within the familiar world, now grown strange, or to a parallel and normally hidden world, is a powerful intensification of the licence to 'irresponsible talk'. The sheer distance of this imagined environment makes possible an even greater range of styles and identities. But perhaps the most liberating thing about such literature is the sense conveyed that the 'normal' world, the habitual ways in which life is structured and control exercised, is not so self-evident that we can't think ourselves around its edges. The child learns to look with a curious, even sceptical, eye at the everyday, ready to ask what are its non-negotiable bits, what are matters of convention or even distortion. What aspects of persons, objects, feelings, relations (landscapes, for that matter) look the same even when some of the ordinary ground rules are shifted? And, in imagining other sorts of beings, other sorts of agents, where, if at all, do we recognise a gap opening up between *that* kind of life and ours? At what point does a peculiarity of behaviour *there* enable us to see for the first time that some aspect of human behaviour *here* is strange and questionable?

Alan Garner is a notable exponent of the parallel world style, his fictions becoming steadily darker and more troubling up to the mid-1970s. Even in the earliest books, though, there is an undertow of disturbing re-visioning. *The Moon of Gomrath* was his second children's fantasy, involving the familiar pattern of children precipitated from the ordinary world into a realm of mythical conflict between strange creatures. Throughout the book, we're made aware of a tantalising oddity, a sort of detachment and chill, in the behaviour of the 'light-elves'; and, fairly well on in the narrative, an explanation is offered by another of the 'fairy' species. The elves fight with bows and arrows, not hand-to-hand, with swords: they can kill at a distance, without seeing the eyes of their victims. ' "You will find in the bows of the lios-alfar much to explain their nature, which was not always as now." '[7] But human beings use bows and arrows, don't they? And guns? So the child reader might ask. Well indeed: now look at human beings again, a bit more carefully. What might the difference be between knowing you're killing a specific person and indiscriminate slaughter? And does the latter make you another kind of person? Were *we* not always as now?

This kind of moral exploration, by way of the play between the familiar and the often outrageously strange, is properly a function of all imaginative writing; and the fictional space as an opportunity for testing styles and identities – even at the level of the suburban soap – goes on being important for anyone trying actively to relate to the world. Even the kind of book popular at 'first reader' level, a vigorous narrating in word and picture of familiar settings and experiences, with some comic dimension or comic distortion (animals doing human things, for instance *Spot goes to School*), is a space for seeing the self and its world afresh. So *that's* what I'm like (or am I?). Being an object to myself, a story for myself – I'm like that,

[7] Alan Garner, *The Moon of Gomrath* (London, 1963), p. 142.

I'm not like that – is the beginning of reflective and imaginative talk, or the irresponsibility that finally shapes us – in ways I'll go on to consider – into choosing agents, answering for ourselves.

This irresponsible talking of children, at whatever level, is set free by the unspoken presence of the habitual, adult-controlled world. You can dispense with the adult in the story precisely because there are adults around to guarantee that the play or the fiction stay within bounds. I shan't suddenly be left stranded, bound to a 'playing' role that I was only testing. The background world allows me to drop out of a fantasy that's become too dangerous or compulsive; I know that, just as I'm discovering the 'normal' world isn't the only possible one, I can also be sure the alternative frame of fantasy isn't the only truth either. Sophisticated older children's or teenagers' fiction can explore the dangers here, to memorable and haunting effect. Some of the abiding power of *Treasure Island* derives from the agonising prolongation of a 'game' of pirates and treasure into painful, sordid and ambiguous reality, with lots of loose ends. The later Alan Garner (*The Owl Service* and the really chilling *Red Shift*) works at the same dangerous edge, as does William Mayne, whose extra-ordinary novel *A Game of Dark* is one of the most searching essays in this genre: in both Mayne and Garner, an emotionally disoriented child, for whom the 'normal' has fractured (parental death, sickness, divorce, traumatic puberty) can become trapped in worlds of mythical force, violent compulsion, that are profoundly frightening and damaging. And fantasy of this kind tells us that fantasy itself relies upon unspoken contracts, on the symbiosis of irresponsible talk with the secure background in which acts *do* have 'ordinary' consequences and fictional identities can be abandoned without emotional shipwreck. At the simplest level, all parents will know the experience of explaining that an over-vivid story (book, video, play, film) is taking place *there* not here, that it has boundaries fixed and controlled by the 'ordinary' world, boundaries for which the adult in some way assumes responsibility: it can be banished without disaster and the familiar world resumed.

The responsibility of the adult in all this is crucial. We are understandably repelled these days at the deliberate cultivating of fiction designed to frighten and subdue children (more worried than some of our ancestors seem to have been); this sort of thing abandons the nurturing responsibility. Perhaps too (with Dickens's Gradgrind in mind, demanding facts and nothing else) we're repelled by an approach that sidelines fantasy and what I've been calling irresponsible talk. More seriously, we are, or should be, shocked and sickened by the picture of thirteen-year-olds conscripted into an army (as in the Iran–Iraq war, and in some of the rebel militias of Africa); by parentless, homeless, criminalised children in the urban streets of Brazil or Guatemala, regularly butchered by police and security forces; by child prostitution – *not* a phenomenon confined to Thailand or Latin America – and sexual abuse. There is a peculiar horror and pathos in children not – as we say – *allowed* to be children. And this was a significant aspect of the wave of nausea that swept Britain in the aftermath of the murder of James Bulger at the hands of two ten-year-olds, and that is echoed every time a child is convicted of killing; these are events that prompt an unusual level of heart-searching by the mass media.

I've used 'we' in the last paragraph, as people do, to

mean the sort of people I expect to be reading these words: those who understand the importance of exercising a responsibility that allows the child room to explore in safety, not to be prematurely committed. But 'we' is always in danger of being a complacent word. There are enough currents around us to suggest that this is in fact a responsibility only dimly understood in its fuller implications, and that the 'we' who believe we are aware of what's involved in the nurture of childhood need to think harder and more systematically about the subject. If in fact we live in an environment in which the definition of the child as a choosing and consuming subject undermines the whole enterprise of nurture, we ought to be asking sharp questions of ourselves and what we take for granted or collude in; so I shall be turning next to look at what kind of 'subject' our culture seems to think a child is.

II

The perception of the child as *consumer* is clearly more dominant than it was a few decades ago. The child is the (usually vicarious) purchaser of any number of graded and variegated packages – that is, of goods designed to stimulate further consumer desires. A relatively innocuous example is the familiar 'tie-in', the association of comics, sweets, toys and so on with a major new film or television serial; the Disney empire has developed this to an unprecedented pitch of professionalism. Rather less innocuous (more obsessive, more expensive) is the computer game designed to lead on to ever more challenging and sophisticated levels. Anything but innocuous is the conscription of children into the fetishistic hysteria of style wars: it is still mercifully rare to murder for a pair of trainers, or to commit suicide because of an inability to keep up with peer group fashion; but what can we say about a marketing culture that so openly feeds and colludes with obsession? What picture of the acting or choosing self is being promoted?

If the child is a consumer, the child is an *economic* subject – even if someone else actually provides the cash, the demand is the child's. And what economic subjects do is commit their capital, limit their options by so doing, take risks for profit or gratification. They make property or assets take on meanings, values, in a pattern of exchange: things become a kind of language. Which is why, as a few metaphysicians have observed, economics is indeed an inescapable part of human business, one of the things we 'just do' as human beings, as makers of meanings. Good: but the rhetoric of consumerism (the arts of advertising) necessarily softens the elements of commitment and risk. It is important to suggest that gain may be had with the minimum of loss. All advertising tends to treat its public as children – tends, that is, to suggest that decisions can be made without cost or risk. This is in the nature of the enterprise (people are seldom attracted by being told about cost or risk): adults can be expected to know something of how this works. But the child targeted by advertising is not likely to be aware of this. He or she becomes an economic subject without the opportunity to recognise those painfully-learned truths about how economic activity commits and limits you. The child as consumer is always a *pseudo*-adult – which may explain something of the confusion and frustration of the child or teenager ('young adult', if you insist) pressured into the obsessive patterns

that arise when economic activity is divorced in imagination from the problems of adult commitment. The most
merciless example of this is, of course, the marketing of
addictive drugs to children; merciless not only to the
children, but in reflecting back to the marketing world the
logic of so much of its 'mainstream' strategy.

The language we use about being an economic subject is
not unlike what we say about being a *sexual* subject. Here
too what we might want to talk about is commitment and
its risks: the whole body becomes, intimately and dangerously, a giver and receiver of meanings or messages, with all
that this implies about limit and potential loss.
Advertising, once again, loves to suggest that being a
sexual subject is fairly unproblematic: the right exercise of
economic choice equips you for a better and fuller range of
sexual opportunity – which is really rather like economic
opportunity. Both kinds of 'market' are presented as
relatively risk-free. Now it is notoriously hard to say just
how far the advertising of children's or even young adults'
goods *deliberately* plays with consciously sexual images; let's
assume, generously, that it does not to any great degree.
The difficulty comes in, more subtly, with a whole vocabulary of choice and gratification, in the unspoken
complexities of rivalry and desire that are not addressed
head-on; the business of learning what it is to be desired,
to be enviable; in the codes that the body is being habit-
uated to, the messages it learns to give. And in any case,
the world of adult advertising is always visibly at hand to
reinforce the message with its own (often imaginatively
and beautifully) erotic idioms. Things are desirable to
make *you* desirable; even before you quite know the nature
of the desire in question, the language is learned. At its

most crass, this can be seen in the postures and gestures of children, girls particularly, in children's talent competitions, beauty contests and so on: the stereotypes of predatory male and seductive female are happily exploited and thought to be rather touching in children of six to eight years old. But the problem is not restricted to this crude setting; as I've hinted, it is everywhere where the display of 'desirability' is fostered in the child, in the very idea of fashion as a proper category for thinking of the child's appearance.

So pressure on the child to be a sexual subject is not simply about the age at which children become sexually active in the usual sense. Cultures, even within our own country, differ and have long differed over this: teenage motherhood (and attendant teenage mortality, often forgotten in this context) has been common enough in many times and places, from mediaeval (especially aristocratic) Europe to parts of modern Asia. When it has suited dynastic or economic ends, the early initiation of sexual activity has seldom been a problem for moralists (whose difficulties have come more with the matter of *controlling* the initiating of sexual activity). The problem is more one of *how* sexual choices are learned and made: how consciously, in what context. Much of our continuing abhorrence of incest seems to rest on the assumption that sustainable adult sexual choices are made more or less impossible if there are *no* areas of our lives and relationships uncoloured by erotic potential. In a weaker form, this is why we establish professional codes for clergy, physicians and others; there needs to be a territory where this question can be put on one side. And incest taboos are like taboos on sexual activity involving children – with which, of course, they frequently coincide. The abusing parent offends us doubly (offends us enough for Freud, famously, to deny the clinical reality of parental incest in the histories of his female patients; still a painfully controversial issue in Freud interpretation – and in modern analytic practice). Both prohibitions effectively claim that there must be regions where the pressure of being object or subject of sexual desire is held off. And, where children are concerned, this has much to do, once again, with the safeguarding of a space where identities can be learned and tested in imagination before commitments have to be made.

The child drawn into sexual activity by the adult has no chance of managing or controlling the meanings his or her body is made to bear. And while loss of some kinds of control is itself *part* of the experience of sexual encounter, we assume that its danger is contained by mutual consent, by the *sharing* of risk. We don't and can't assume that such containment is possible in a radically unequal situation (we know the damage to self-perception that is caused by rape). As for sexual activity *between* children, a similar point holds as for the incest taboo. We are not necessarily faced here with the exploitative inequalities of adult–child sex; but there is the same erosion of a 'space' not dominated by the pressures of erotic desire and choice – and by the vulnerability and uncertainty thus introduced when my body becomes something that may or may *not* be desirable to another. Exactly *when* sexual latency ends may be a less important matter to settle than recognising that there is such a thing as sexual latency, and that it needs serious attention and protection if sexual maturation is in any way to keep step with the whole process of imaginative maturation. If there is no such recognition, or if we have no sense at all of the rationale of according such a recognition, we are culturally guilty of the equivalent of conscripting the teenage guerrilla; not to mention the child prostitute.

The point could be expressed most simply by saying that children need to be free of the pressure to make adult choices if they are ever to *learn* how to make adult choices. For them to be free for irresponsibility and fantasy, free from the commitments of purchasing and consuming, is for them to have time to absorb what is involved in adult choice. Failure to understand this is losing the very *concept* of childhood. But it is just this failure to understand that is evident in the slippage in our public images and practices towards treating the child as a consumer, an economic and erotic subject, in ways that obscure the whole business of *learning to choose*. And the loss in question here is sharpened by wider economic pressures. We (the liberal-minded) may and do complain about the pervasively middle-class atmosphere of much 'classic' children's literature (including all the examples so far cited here). But this feature of the literature has a lot to do with the bald fact that poverty is a poor environment for protected spaces of freedom, or for having time to learn through unpressured play. It may well be that some of what goes into our concept of childhood derives from a very specific Western 'moment' after the Industrial Revolution, when significant numbers of children among the new middle classes were relieved from the direct pressure of contributing to an agrarian or cottage-industry economy, and, quite simply, had time on their hands. And while every culture has the notion of protecting the young in some important aspects, Western bourgeois families undoubtedly prolonged this period, creating new markets for education and entertainment. Be that as it may, the *decline* of industrial society, the steady growth of a sector of the population excluded from the processes of production and wealth creation, brings new problems for childhood. In areas of major economic depression, especially urban deprivation, the environment is commonly one in which material poverty and the pervasive images of consumerism sit side by side; there is little to soften the pressures of those images, while at the same time there are few straight-forward or legitimate ways to gratify the desires nurtured by them. Thus the drug economy flourishes and small-scale crime is almost too common to notice. Furthermore, this is an environment in which adult stress and depression – often intensified in, though not exclusive to, the lone parent household – limits the ability and willingness of parents to secure pressure-free space for children, or to provide models of adult choice – if only because the range of real options available, economic, political, even sexual, is narrow. It is an environment in which heroic efforts are made by many adults, parents and teachers alike, to sustain the possibility of experiencing childhood in the ways already discussed; but the dice are heavily loaded against them.

In this context – but also in many that are supposedly more 'privileged' – the effect of blurring the boundaries of childhood and limiting the choices of adults is a situation in which adults revert to childlike behaviour, uncommitted and fantasy-driven, and children and adults can come to see themselves as *rivals* in a single arena of competition. Sexually, socially, economically, the child may seem to be bidding for the same goods, and the difference between a child's and an adult's desires is not grasped. In another much-publicised scandal of 1993, a mother who left her eleven-year-old daughter alone in the house while she disappeared for a holiday, spoke of this almost in terms of punishment for the child's pert or flirtatious manner ('a right little madam'). More than one commentator remarked on the implication that the child was being presented as a competitor in 'desirability'. Regressive adult and precocious child meet in a situation where the child's actual vulnerability can be overlooked until too late, a situation which is thus fraught with possibilities of violence.

The 'safest' adult to have around is one who is aware of having *grown* – one, that is, who knows in his or her own experience how transitions are made from one sort of choosing to another (which also means one who hasn't forgotten what it is *like* to be a child). A society that is generally disabled in its choice-making will produce childish adults, bad at the nurture of children because they are not secure in their adult freedoms. There are some paradoxes here, of course. It is not unknown for totalitarian societies to channel quite high levels of creative energy into child-rearing and education; there were aspects of the educational system of the old Soviet Union, at some moments in its history, that were not completely contemptible. But in the long run, unintelligent political education will produce either conformism or cynicism – or a debilitating mixture of the two – and will undo any good that emerges elsewhere in the system (as in the Soviet Union again). If people are not developing into real political subjects, there is a major area of adult freedom that remains uncultivated.

There is also a rather different problem, accentuated in

the past couple of decades. Learning to *assert* ones claims, needs and dignities as an adult has become a matter of immense cultural importance; and it can be an aspect of learning how to foster the needs and dignities of children effectively and without resentment. The Neanderthal Right quite regularly blames feminism for the collapse of the family and the menaces to childhood in our culture. But the woman who is left unfree to negotiate economic and other choices in a society where choice overall is more varied and more pressured is, if my earlier argument was right, more at risk of regression and of rivalry with a child. There are so often chains of violence and abuse transmitted from the powerless, childish male adult in a situation of deprivation to the still more powerless woman and on to the child; and these are chains unlikely to be broken without a clear feminist analysis of cycles of violence and powerlessness – as well as the broader economic transformations needed. To say this is also to recognise the need for critical work on male self-perception, especially the ways in which economic powerlessness reinforces the regressive aspects of 'standard' male behaviour and male bonding – machismo as a response to poverty or status uncertainty. The problem arises – and it is a problem we shall be returning to more than once in these pages – of the point at which the assertion of right becomes a less-than-adult claim to nothing more than access to an open market, an assertion of the right to compete. When that happens, we are back to the destructive situation of adult and child in potential competition for limited goods, losing the *distance* between adult and non-adult desire that preserves the dignity of both.

The implication of all this is that if children are to be

allowed to be children, we have to ask about what prevents adults being adults. Not only parents, but adults in general, adults in their social organisation and their political choices, have to grasp what is involved in becoming responsible for the nurture and induction into human society of new human subjects in process of formation. A recent book by a Roman Catholic writer meditating on Rembrandt's great painting of the return of the Prodigal Son concludes with reflections on the difficulty of taking up the role of the parent in the group depicted, compared with the relative ease of identifying with the older or the younger son: 'Do I want to be not just the one who is being forgiven, but also the one who forgives; not just the one who is being welcomed home, but also the one who welcomes home?'[8] A society that pushes us towards dependent and frustrated patterns of behaviour will not enable adults to be 'at home' with their limits and their choices in a way that makes it possible to welcome or nurture those who are bound to be dependent, who are still learning their own freedom. How then do we, how are we encouraged to, understand the nature of adult choice in our environment?

III

We are told often enough that our society is set more and more to maximise choice. Is it, then, one in which adult choices are better grasped and more easily possible? The signs are not encouraging, if we take the signs to include

[8] Henri Nouwen, *The Return of the Prodigal Son. A Story of Homecoming* (London, 1992), p. 115 (p. 122 in the 1994 edition).

the marks of alienation – juvenile crime and adult abuse, the growth of a non-working population with no stake in society, the chaos in personal and familial relations in areas of deprivation (and elsewhere), and the general confusion and bitterness over methods and goals in state education. If we think of adult choice as the choice of 'somewhere to live', settling on options that allow us to act more freely and intelligently by giving us definition, giving us graspable material to work on, we have to reckon with the fact that such choice closes off avenues by giving my life definition, a definition it can only have by refusing certain openings. I am changed by my choices, and I can't simply revert to the position I had before – which is itself a position already defined and limited by choices. Real choice both expresses and curtails freedom – or rather it should lead us further and further away from a picture of choice that presupposes a blank will looking out at a bundle of options like goods on a supermarket shelf.

And here originates a good deal of our trouble. Is this in fact how choice is presented to us? If we think back to what's been said about the culture of advertising, it is more or less in the nature of the beast that the 'choices' here put before us are presented to an *abstract* will or personality, to nobody-in-particular; they address, of course, bundles of instincts, fears and desires, sometimes the instinct or prejudice of a group or class, but never a person with a history or a specific kind of vulnerability. Advertising could not work otherwise, and the best we can hope for is an education that lets us notice what is going on, how advertising 'constructs' its abstract consumers, its impersonal but impassioned audience. But what about other areas where the rhetoric of 'choice' is powerful at the moment? I want to look briefly at two such areas, asking how far our current practice really looks to or equips *adult* choosing: the parent's 'right to choose' in respect of children's education, and the woman's 'right to choose' as presented in contemporary debates about abortion. I am aware that this is a contentious juxtaposition.

For a decade and a half, we have been consistently told by government that the protection of 'parental choice' in educational matters is one of the most fundamental imperatives in a proper education policy. The appeal of this is genuinely powerful, because it has a ring of altruism – wanting what's best for a growing generation – at the same time as having a comforting ring of tribalism – wanting what's best for our own. The harder you look at these two sorts of appeal, however, the more difficult it is to hold them together in terms of *choice*. I want to be able to choose a 'better' education for my child, and so I must require educational institutions to furnish me with information about their relative success or failure; without this, there is not much sense in speaking at all about the right to choose, and it is quite logical that a policy stressing such a right should involve pressure on schools to provide a copious flow of information about their performance (test results, league tables and so on). But who in such circumstances *chooses* a school identified as 'failing' (to use the current jargon)? Just possibly, a parent with a strong commitment to – say – education in a multi-ethnic setting might say that it's more important to equip a child to live acceptingly in a diverse society than to secure a particular cluster of qualifications, and might accordingly opt for a school with higher diversity and lower average examination results. But that is a consciously risky business, and it is a bold parent who is sure enough about this to jeopardise a child's possible vocational/professional future. Those doing so are obviously *choosing*, though on the basis of different criteria of excellence: they are not choosing what they see as failure. But more generally it should be self-evident that the notion of failure here already begins to limit the supposed availability of choice. To attract custom, a school must 'succeed'; and this almost invariably means selection by academic promise. Some will be rejected, and will end up in schools by definition less 'successful'; and who wants to choose them? Yet they will be the only possibilities for some parents. The language of choice is beginning to look far from innocent.

If the parent (on the child's behalf) is a consumer and the school a provider or producer, the school competes in a finite market, a market where one producer's gain is another's loss (there is not a lot that a rival producer can do in this context to 'diversify' to avoid failure). A school's excellence, measured in the apparently straightforward ways specified in present policy, is bound up with its capacity to attract customers away from competitors. Within a finite geographical area, this becomes a means of attracting not only 'custom' but resources – local enthusiasm, the support of parents with managerial and fundraising skills; and so a model such as this necessarily involves a spiral of failure for the less successful competitors, and the consequence diminution of *real* choice for some parents. And a parallel spiral is set up among consumers: the 'successful' school can, to some extent, negotiate conditions, intensify its selectivity, setting terms that only a certain percentage of applicants can satisfy – a necessary move, since the school itself is a finite system whose resources have to be economically deployed. Parents can become caught in anxiety about their ability to negotiate with the school to establish the viability of their choice. The end result is a situation in which certain schools and parents are effectively *without* choice, because resources are slanted in one direction by the imposition of uniform standards of excellence, and the experience of choice for the more fortunate is shadowed by anxieties about how to meet increasingly stringent conditions for the exercise of that choice.

In short, the language of choice applied to the educational system is deceptive. By concentrating our attention on parental freedom to choose the 'best' available provision, it distorts both our moral and our more narrowly educational perceptions. It encourages us to ignore the context and effects of such choice, nudging us insistently away from the awkward question of how everyone's supposed right to choose could be honoured in a framework like this. It also encourages us to assume that there is a single and fairly easily measurable standard of success in education. In both respects, the language of choice helps us to postpone or set aside questions about education as something that has to do with expressing and fostering a *corporate* responsibility – the shared responsibility of inducting children into a social environment with at least some common values, and the providing of what is needed to understand and question that environment in terms of its success in embodying values. Since we currently don't seem to know, as a society, what we want to 'induct' children into or what we consider to be the foundation of our society's moral legitimacy (that is, what makes this society worth belonging to or defending), it isn't surprising that we take refuge in treating education as the process of purchasing blocks of training material. When our consciences are particularly tender on all this, we consider adding a block called 'moral education'. This will inevitably have a somewhat abstract feel to it – as does the valiant but rather elusive document on 'Values and Education in the Community' produced in 1996 for the School Curriculum and Assessment Authority. And it is a gloomy fact that left and right often mouth the same clichés here. By accepting the polarisation of 'academic' and 'vocational', by applying simplistic tests of relevance or accessibility, educationalists on both sides of the political divide can successfully bracket out the most fundamental issue: how are people to acquire a language in which they can *think* about the character of their society? For that requires both a fluency in the traditions, even the mythology, of the society you're in, *and* a confidence sufficient to test and challenge its inconsistencies or deceptions. There was once a powerful socialist vision of education as learning tradition so as to make it a critical tool; but voices like those of Raymond Williams, Richard Hoggart or E. P. Thompson are none too audible on the left these days.

'Choice' in education is a term that must be stripped of its false innocence. The prevailing use of the word conceals a deep scepticism about the whole idea of education as serving a common interest, providing a language for public debate and moral wrangling. Choice in this context looks remarkably like the successful assertion of *will* when you analyse it; and the supposed goodness of free choice in education is not very different from the desirability of my being able to defend and sustain my interest – albeit through another party, the child, whose interests are seen as an extension of mine. Now where the assertion of my will is simply about matters of relative indifference to other agents and their interests, if it is indeed like selecting a brand from the shelf, it does not seem too problematic – though campaigns about South African produce or Nestlé have opened our eyes to the fact that even supermarket choices may have moral and political connotations. The truth is that very few indeed of our human options are like that. I said earlier that 'real' choices both express and limit freedom; if we are encouraged to ignore the elements of limit, the limiting of myself and, just as importantly, the limiting and determining of someone else's horizon, we end up in fantasy or confusion or both. We will not be making adult choices and we will not be taking responsibility – in the educational context – for inducting children into a properly *social* world: we will be deploying them, conscripting them, into thinly concealed conflicts over whose interest will be allowed to prevail. To bolt on components of 'moral education' to a system whose *methods* already communicate a particular moral message (conflict and rivalry) is not likely to help. Furthermore, part of the strategy of this conflict of interest is the refusal to articulate what's going on, the truth that choice for one group is preserved or defended at the cost of the freedom of others to choose what they want or need. An educational strategy that conceals this is not going to induct children into any lively sense of goods and goals that are not sectional, interests that are not local or in some way tribal.

The rhetoric of choice as a controlling good in education is one of the factors that makes for a society profoundly inept in handling adult self-determination and responsibility. We don't particularly want to know how our choices make a difference – to the possibilities open to others, and thus to our relations with those others, and thus to our own longer-term possibilities. The involvement of our own good or interest with that of others is a theme that will recur frequently in this book. If we lose the edge to our thinking about choice, lose the awareness that choice means loss, and that the morally taxing questions are about how that loss is 'distributed', it is natural enough that we lose the awareness of the distinction between how adults choose and how children choose. We end up with the child as consumer, economic and erotic, and thus as potential rival. We end up assuming that human beings do not have to *learn* to choose; will triumphs over the messy and time-consuming business of reflection, the thinking through of our relationships and dependencies. And one consequence is the loss of an integral understanding of what childhood is, with the corrupting and violent results which are becoming familiar.

Education is one example among many of the debasement of choice that has become current, the now almost universal reduction of agent to consumer. Similar points could be made about the encouragement given to cable television, let alone the 'consumerising' of primary health care. But these are quite familiar themes; instead of exploring the fairly obvious parallels with education, I want to look at a far more complex and contentious example – the use of 'pro-choice' as a designation for the position of those in favour of liberalised abortion laws. One or two preliminary points had better be cleared away before further discussion. I accept that in anything other than strict modern theological terms, there is a widespread uncertainty as to when one can begin to speak of an identifiable *individual* in the first few weeks of a pregnancy, and that this uncertainty colours the emotional responses of many who would be unhappy with unrestricted access to abortion for women at any stage of pregnancy. I accept also that the termination of a pregnancy is not necessarily in all circumstances the worst possible moral option, even though I consider this to be the termination of a human life. And, like many others, I am sickened by the rhetoric and practice of anti-abortion activists whose respect for human life turns out to be curiously selective, activists who are prepared to threaten or kill surgeons involved in abortion, or simply those who see no contradiction between their views on abortion and their endorsement of militarism. I am genuinely puzzled by political parties, governments or churches that appear to find a greater moral problem in abortion than in the manufacture, marketing and use of indiscriminate weaponry, from cluster bombs and poison gas to nuclear warheads. Confusion, dishonesty and misplaced dogmatism in this area have lowered the moral credibility of any critical questioning of liberal orthodoxies on abortion in the eyes of many, if not most, articulate citizens of the North Atlantic world.

But this does not alter the ambiguity of 'pro-choice' as the designation of a moral position. 'Not the Church, not the State, Women must decide their fate' is a well-known slogan; and what it appeals to is in fact a deeply moral perception, that any system programmatically denying to someone the liberty to become 'subjects of their own history', authors in some degree of their destiny, is indefensible in moral terms, *precisely* because it rules out certain groups or persons as possible candidates for making what I've been calling adult choices. However, what the slogan silences or encourages us to ignore is that the moral world is not very satisfactorily defined in terms of individuals 'deciding their fates' in a vacuum. No one at all 'decides their fate' in the sense that their choices shape only their own lives and possibilities, or that *only* their choices shape their lives and possibilities. The question that arises, as with the rhetoric of educational choice, is whether the word 'choice' itself translates simply as the freedom to protect your own interests at the inevitable expense of other makers of choices.

This is where the complications begin in earnest. We don't treat the foetus as a real subject, a maker of choices, it is argued. It would be absurd to speak of its 'freedom' being violated. Can we therefore speak of its 'interests' in the same breath as those of an independent human agent? We call it 'it', because its human identity is still unformed as far as our adult perspective is concerned: we haven't until recently been in a position to know its sex before birth. We don't treat the issue of a miscarriage as a human corpse – though we feel differently about a stillbirth or a very late miscarriage, a point well made by Mary Gordon in a careful and nuanced 'pro-choice' essay.[9] Surely here if anywhere the language of free choice as a good for the adult subject can be used without too deep a shadow?

This would be an easier argument to sustain if we did not at the same time treat the foetus as having 'claims' of its own – for which purpose, the textbook will begin to write

[9] Mary Gordon, *Good Boys and Dead Girls and Other Essays* (New York, 1991), pp. 140–1.

about the *child* rather than the *foetus*. When we discourage the pregnant woman from smoking or alcohol consumption, when we make recommendations about exercise or lifestyle, we treat her as someone morally constrained by interests not completely defined by her. She may, outside pregnancy, 'innocently' choose to indulge in practices that may undermine health: only when these affect others – smoking in a non-smoking railway carriage, alcohol abuse causing violence or criminal neglect – does the moral temperature go up. A choice we may not applaud but are content to tolerate becomes a more public matter. And it seems as if the relation of mother to foetus is morally nearer to this public territory than to the liberty of an individual to treat her body as she chooses; her choices have become recognised as setting limits on some other subject's possibilities. We may not regard the issue of miscarriage as if it were the body of a named individual; yet we do regard it as having a place within a network of human interests, as a notional partner in possible conversations, as carrying the particular charge of being an object of love.

Possible conversations: but surely this is different from the relationships we have to *independent* others? The foetus exists, for at least the greater part of the gestation period, in a state of absolute physical dependence upon the mother: it can have no life outside the womb. What does it mean to treat it as a real 'other'? It means, at the very least, to recognise a coherent life-system which, however closely dependent upon a 'host' system, possesses a relationship to its entire environment that is not the same as that of the 'host' system. Indeed, the dependence itself is a mark of that difference; we cannot avoid speaking of

41

relation here, in a way we do not and cannot speak of my relation to my finger or my kidneys. Is this enough for real *moral* otherness? As one or two recent commentators, notably Fergus Kerr,[10] have observed, we should be careful about the possible implications of saying 'No' to this. If we want to say that there are pieces of evidence that can help us decide whether or not we give this or that biological phenomenon the status of person, we run severe risks. If 'moral otherness' depends on the right accumulation of properties on the part of a putatively human system, we shall always risk enumerating or categorising those properties in a way that rules out some controversial claimants. People regularly, when they try to specify in this area, refer to qualities such as rationality, capacity to take responsibility for actions or respond coherently to stimuli, to participate in communicative or meaningful action in some way; and such suggestions leave us with a nest of difficulties about the status of the newborn, the senile, the severely handicapped in mind or even body (where communication skills are impaired). Just why are we licensed to consider them as moral others, endowed with interests comparable to ours, claiming access to a good like ours? The question is hard to answer; but, despite the robust conclusions of one or two recent philosophers, like Peter Singer, the plain denial of the granting of such a status to, for example, a newborn infant, seems to be counter-intuitive.

But, it could be replied, in any theoretically doubtful cases like these we – concretely and physically – recognise an organism existing in its own right, sufficiently like our

---

[10] Fergus Kerr, *Theology after Wittgenstein* (Oxford, 1986), pp. 176–7.

own independent organic existence to be a plausible sharer of our interests; not so with the foetus, or at least not before a certain point in pregnancy. Again, though, is this so clear? Pro-choice activists are quite right to say that technology has in some ways made their position emotionally harder, because of the ready availability of photographic images, variously enhanced, of the foetus. When abortion legislation was last debated in the British parliament, a 'pro-life' group sent MPs lifesize models of twenty-week foetuses, and much outrage was expressed by campaigners on the other side. Similarly, when the *New Statesman* a couple of years earlier carried on its cover the photograph of a well-developed foetus, there was a good deal of angry correspondence: this, it was said, could only play into the hands of the 'pro-life' agitation. The anger is revealing, and rather disturbing. It acknowledges the significance of sheer instinctive recognition, 'animal' recognition we could almost say, in responding to something as a moral other; and it implies the desirability of learning to suppress, ignore or minimise such an element in the forming of a rational moral response, the desirability of – in some circumstances – arguing people out of these reactions. But once that has been granted, houseroom has been given to a very ambiguous principle – that we should be taught to question what I have called 'animal' recognition. This in effect raises the question once again of the possibility of criteria for 'counting' as a human being, and whether there is a plausible way of artic-ulating or listing these. But if there is, we are clearly into the territory where the claims of some putatively human organisms is to be decided by others unilaterally: the question has become one of power, the profound power of definition. The power to decide the human claims of others is, of course, precisely what feminism rightly rebels against – the long and shameful history of educating people to ignore, distort or minimise certain kinds of biological community and the recognitions that are or should be bound up with them. The history of patriarchy – not to mention racism – shows that such a project is by no means impossible.

Yes, but perhaps this is only a back-projection of the form of the second-trimester foetus on to the barely determinate 'streak' of genetic material that exists at the beginning of a pregnancy. So the objector might respond, and with some justification. The 'pro-life' use of images from later in gestation might reasonably be challenged as giving the impression that the embryo of the first weeks of pregnancy is already *visibly* a 'small person'. Yet the structure of the embryo is what it is in virtue of what it will develop into: it is not a different *kind* of organism from the second-trimester foetus, and what happens to it determines what becomes of foetus, child and adult in all kinds of ways. As the 'pro-choice' advocate insists, there is a long and complex process going on even between conception and the formation of what we can call an identifiable nervous system; we can easily be hurried to a conclusion when the obvious is pointed out – that the qualities we instinctively associated with 'being a person' seem to be present in the pregnant woman and absent in the contents of her womb during the first weeks of gestation. But if the real issue is not 'counting as a person', qualifying to join the company of fully-fledged possessors of personal rights, but simply being a moral other, the possessor of interests not reducible to mine, the case is not so clear. As Fergus Kerr notes, almost in passing,[11] the recognition of this rests on a recognition of our own fundamentally animal condition, as material systems involved in varying kinds of material relationship to an environment, relationships of dependence and interdependence. The pro-choice argument may say, 'Granted there is an area of uncertainty, there is surely some clarity about the ends of the spectrum – genetic streak and quasi-infant (third trimester, say)'; but the point has to be pondered that this is a spectrum extending between different *levels* of dependence and biological organisation: at no point can we mark a transition from one *kind* of life to another.

These considerations are not meant to settle the fiercely debated question of the law's role in all this; my concern is more with the kind of moral discourse within this debate that exhibits disturbing features, a simplifying of the notion of free choice into the terms of a purely individual good. Reversion to a pre-1967 situation would only be attractive, even morally defensible, in the context of a massive reconstruction of attitudes to childcare and nurture, to the professional lives of childbearing women, the availability of other forms of fertility control to women, and many other things besides. The entire question is also badly in need of informing from the standpoint of those who have examined the psychologies of pregnancy and childbearing: a recent book on this makes great play of the fact that, like it or not, the *relation*

[11] Ibid. p. 177: 'Paradoxically enough, the more animal we remember ourselves to be [that is, the more we move away from defining ourselves as autonomous reasoners first and foremost], the weightier the theological objections to abortion and embryo experimentation might become.'

between mother and conceptus is from the first precisely that, a relation, with all that that involves of projection and the need to free the other from projection, negative and positive. But this seems an issue worth spending time on, if only because we have now reached a situation where most of the onus appears to lie with those arguing the moral otherness, the distinct and irreducible interest of the unborn – a situation reinforced by current trends and practice in genetics involving the 'breeding' of human embryos for research. It is now far easier and more fashionable to defend the moral otherness of animals, or even of the inanimate environment, than to persuade people of the appropriateness of defending unborn humans in this way, although there is intense *clinical* pressure to identify the foetus as a quasi-child whose welfare the mother is obliged to foster. The *reductio ad absurdum* of would-be legal definitions of foetal rights only serves to pinpoint the bizarre confusion British and American society tolerates in this area, where the defenders of the moral status of veal calves and rainforests seem to find no problem with the moral invisibility of certain categories of embryonic humans.

But there may be a point capable of being owned by both sides of the abortion debate, a point bringing us back towards the main argument of this chapter. 'Pro-choice' is a slogan that can very easily be a recommendation to *ignore* something, just as it is in the educational world. By treating the availability of 'choice' in a situation as *the* moral issue of decisive importance, it can again collude in the reduction of ethics to the question of who is able more successfully to defend their interest against others: ethics as a conflict about power. Feminist ethics has had a vastly important role in unmasking the ways in which supposedly 'disinterested' talk about ethics, sexual, economic or familial, has an unacknowledged agenda that is to do with the control of some human beings by others. It is a bit of a paradox that the discussion of abortion, quick to suspect a patriarchal anxiety to control women's power in relation to their own fertility, so easily sidesteps the problems of power that lie in the shadow of 'pro-choice' rhetoric – if you are prepared to grant some level of genuine moral otherness to the unborn. The very rhetoric itself does less than justice to the acute sense of the tragic experienced at some stage by many women opting for abortion, who may be haunted by an otherness denied, even if they stand by their decision.

IV

If we are able to demythologise the goodness of choice as the affirmation of the consumer's will, we may have learned something of value in understanding the relation of child and adult, the main burden of this opening essay. Protecting the human young from some of the pressures of adult choice implies a recognition that such choice is weighty, potentially tragic, bound up with unseen futures for the agent and other agents. To learn about this, I have argued, requires a space for fantasy, a licence for imagination, where gradually the consequences, the self-defining knots, of adult choice can be figured, fingered, experimented with. To look at the child as economic and sexual consumer is to flatten the landscape of our own adulthood, to make universal a model of choice that is at best partial and trivial; and also to treat the child as a market rival, confirming that ambivalent strain of rivalry that both energises and skews culture. It is, of course, possible to say that 'protecting' the child is again about power or control; but if it is true that the child doesn't come into the world fully equipped for moral self-definition, if the very language of selfhood has to be *learned* as we grow, we are not in the situation of one adult group claiming the right to set the definitions of another. We are rather trying to equip a child to *exercise* power, to hold off unequal and deeply damaging contests of power while the child is still acquiring it. It may be said that it is almost impossible to establish a clear line between legitimate nurture and oppressive control; and this is indisputably true. But the difficulty is not to be dissolved by denying its presence and complexity. It is in negotiating the risks here that we discover a good deal about our own adulthood, and the denial of the difficulty is a denial of the very realities of mature choosing.

Because of the risk and difficulty here, we are going to be very tempted by the flattened landscapes of 'consumer' choice. It fits well into a political landscape where responsibility for the interest of the other is consistently obscured. The consideration of the fate of our children is one of the few areas in which, it seems, we are still capable of being frightened back into reflection on such responsibility. Nearly everyone in our society with any direct involvement with children experiences directly and painfully the sheer *unsafety* of the child today. Half-defined terrors hide around every corner, scarring events like the Dunblane massacre leave us both terrified and helpless. But the fact that the greatest incidence of child abuse occurs in

48

the home, or in a supposedly 'controlled' environment (sexual abuse in Children's Homes) ought to give us pause. Some damage to the corporate psyche seems to be taking place, some loss of the burden and gift of nurture, for this to be quite so prevalent. What if children need to be protected from contemporary adults, quite simply? Because contemporary adults have abandoned their role and trust? That is an absurdly extreme idea; but does it contain enough to worry us constructively?

At the end of the day, the problem goes deeper than we have been able to probe in this chapter. The reluctance to think about nurture and the learning of choice is fundamentally, I suggest, a reluctance to think about the role of *time* in the formation of identities. The style obsessions of our day help to reinforce the idea that identities can be purchased and discarded; the fascination of some with virtual reality and cyberspace illustrates vividly the attractions of a post-humanist milieu in which the closed options, self-determinations and irreversible sequences of an older sense of human identity are challenged or regarded as transcended. I want to look at some of the attendance issues from other perspectives later on. But one of the points worth registering at this stage is that an incapacity to see people as *produced*, formed in their biology and psychology by the passage of time, implies a fixity in our perceptions of each other that is potentially very troubling. A world of timeless consuming egos, adopting and discarding styles of self-presentation and self-assertion, is a social as well as a philosophical shambles.

To recognise a cultural loss and a cultural crisis is (notoriously) not much of a step to solving it; but it is something. It gives a perspective from which to question public policies and debates – even though the underlying issues are not easily capable of being resolved by planning alone. At present in the United Kingdom, education is suffering a steady attrition of resources and imagination, and is at every level under pressure to give priority to narrowly functional concerns; it is treated politically as a consumer good to be marketed to parents or students. In the long run, this is bound to weaken any sense of corporate responsibility and public intelligence. It is not that responsibility isn't learned and exercised by individuals and families in continuing tradition, despite what goes on in the educational establishment; but how is the vision of the individual or family to be supported and enlarged? St Augustine's passing observation in *The City of God* [12] that the household learns its values from the city, is worth pondering, however odd it may sound to modern ears. And since our attitudes to education are only a part of the general trend towards the sovereignty of market metaphors, we have to continue to train ourselves and each other to challenge the supposed *obviousness* of such metaphors – indeed, to expose the fact that, applied to areas like education and healthcare, they are singularly bad metaphors. If we can free ourselves from at least this bit of slavery, we might be able more robustly to challenge the narrow models of choice that fuel the market metaphor.

This investigation raises some further questions about the kinds of bonds and conventions that actively pull against the sovereignty of market rhetoric, that construct the self as something other than an abstract consuming machine. It will not do to treat these problems about

[12] Augustine, *The City of God*, Book xix, chapter 16.

choice and childhood as simply arising from the faulty options of individuals: that would only be to *illustrate* the problem itself, by treating the morally interesting question as one about individuals exercising freedom in a vacuum. To say that things go wrong because free agents happen to select the wrong one of a set of possible courses of definite action is to assume that options and actions are not significantly constrained by the individual and collective past, or by the choices of others.

Take a familiar example, a relevant one in the context of this chapter. The protection of the imaginative space of childhood obviously needs a background of security, adult availability and adult consistency; a background of constantly shifting adult relationships, with the investment of energy involved in starting, sustaining and extricating oneself from relationships, doesn't, on the face of it, sound like a promising basis. The tempting conclusion is, as some enthusiastic 'communitarians' would argue, that divorce should be made more difficult in law, so as to guarantee greater stability in the family. Unfortunately (as anyone with any experience in counselling troubled couples will ruefully confirm) this is precisely what can *not* be guaranteed by multiplying legal obstacles. To make it legally harder to make a wrong choice is still to see the important factor as the individual's will: restrain that will by legal force, and all will be well, the choice will not be made. But this would be to ignore the manifold factors, interior and exterior, that can cause an option for divorce (like an option for abortion) to appear attractive. Somehow the matter has to be addressed at another level, in a wider context: what are the social supports for a marriage or other committed partnership? What level of practical assistance (from paternity leave to crèche facilities to professional advice in emergency) are readily available? And – elusive but important – what messages about fidelity, patience, the formation of persons in time, are being given out by the enveloping culture? In short, what do we, as a society, think and do about sustaining bonds of different sorts? This will not prevent a specific wrong choice, or resolve at a stroke the mess and suffering of the broken family; but without this sort of question, no real resolution is possible. We shall only compound the suffering.

Present trends in reacting to marital breakdown lay a fair bit of emphasis on the importance of *conciliation* services – that is, services which, while not necessarily aiming at the full restoration of a partnership, offer the possibility of working at and thinking through reasonable common aims for a couple separating – financial fairness, proper provision for children, and so on. This is in fact a good example of a process in which the sovereignty of individual will is appropriately challenged, so that a potentially endless spiral of competitive struggle is checked and negotiation becomes possible. In a conciliation process, everyone has to allow that their initial account of what they need or want is *revisable*; and this is at least a small part of the construction of a social environment that contains or manages conflict. But, as we have noted, it is just that kind of environment that seems to be under serious threat these days; and it is no use asking how we are to mend our losses in the area of the experience of childhood as sketched in this chapter without looking at other and wider losses, losses in respect of what I shall be calling 'charity' in our social world.

2

Charity

John Bossy's *Christianity in the West, 1400–1700* is a vivid, learned and delightful portrait of a period of major change in Church and society; and one of the many original ways that Bossy offers of measuring change is through the shift that took place in the meanings of certain words – and, indeed, to the whole way in which *meaning* itself was thought about. Following Michel Foucault, he observes that, at the earlier limit of the period he is studying, meanings are about resemblances and continuities: the universe is a vast system of cross-reference, and for something to be significant, to communicate a content, is for it to share in the 'field' of reference of something else. 'In [this] earlier universe things participated with each other, with the language which described them, and the persons who spoke of them.'[1] Thus, in the case of one of the words whose meaning lurches dramatically away from its earlier course, '"Charity" in 1400 meant the state of Christian love or simple affection which one was in or out of regarding one's fellows; an occasion or body of people seeking to embrace that state; the love of God, in both directions.' By the latter

---

[1] John Bossy, *Christianity in the West, 1400–1700* (Oxford, 1985), p. 169.

end of Bossy's period, it had come to mean 'an optimistic judgement about the good intentions of others' (as in a 'charitable' interpretation of something), a benefaction for the needy (a person can now be 'dependent on charity'), or the institutional means of continuing such a benefaction (*a* charity, in the modern sense of what the Charity Commissioners concern themselves with).[2] The word has ceased to mean anything much like a *bond*, except in the weak sense in which two or more people may have 'charitable' attitudes towards each other; and the very bondedness, the continuity, between the mediaeval meanings has been practically destroyed.

Much of Bossy's book is in fact about charity in the older sense, the sense still preserved in the 'love and charity towards your neighbours' of the Book of Common Prayer. Charity is the manifestation of what Bossy calls 'the social miracle'[3] – the extraordinary processes by which sectional loyalties were from time to time interrupted and overcome by a sense of integration, of belonging with an entire social body extending far beyond one's choice or one's affiliations of interest and 'natural' loyalty. In terms of institutions, the immense popularity of fraternities in the later Middle Ages witnesses to the desire to move beyond kinship loyalties and hierarchical structures towards a state of highly formalised friendship, a reciprocal and egalitarian community. 'In some cases', Bossy writes, 'the incorporation of persons of differing status was a formal object of the fraternal institution.'[4] This was cemented by common ceremonies which invariably

---

[2] On the history of organised charity, see Ian Williams, *The Alms Trade. Charities, Past, Present and Future* (London, 1989), esp. chapters 1 and 2.

[3] Bossy, *Christianity in the West*, chapter 4.

[4] Ibid. p. 58.

included regular celebratory meals, but which also stressed that essential building-block of social civility, the formalising of mutually respectful and affectionate greeting. These voluntary bodies, whose primary purpose was simply social bonding outside the family structure, could and did play significant roles in controlling factional strife in (for example) Italian cities; in some areas, what we think of as the parochial system in the Church actually developed later than the fraternity system. The fraternity *was* the worshipping community, responsible for organising liturgical provision and pastoral care.[5] And in terms of *events*, 'charity' was honoured and secured by major public festivals – notably, by the end of the Middle Ages, the summer holiday of Corpus Christi; though there were other significant occasions on which the public renunciation or transcendence of violent rivalry was more or less obligatory. At Corpus Christi, however, the 'social miracle' was firmly and explicitly rooted in the entire history of God's dealings with the world, through the medium of the mystery plays in England and elsewhere, and in the public processions displaying the Sacrament of Christ's body. What is shown here is not only the meaning of social bondedness in relation to the act of God and the worshipping community, but – to return to the point made earlier about the very nature of meaning – the way in which that social meaning works, by a kind of 'nesting' of frames of reference within each other: the social body, the Church as Body of Christ, the sacramental

[5] Ibid. pp. 62–3.
[6] Ibid. pp. 71–2; cf. the now classical study by Miri Rubin, *Corpus Christi. The Eucharist in Late Mediaeval Culture* (Cambridge, 1991).

presence of Christ's body in the Eucharist; a subtle crossing and recrossing of the boundaries between fields of discourse.[6]

What charity involves in this context is above all the opportunity for suspending relationships characterised by competition, rivalry. The civilities of the fraternity – greeting, meeting and eating, as Bossy nicely puts it[7] – direct energy away from competition towards the maintenance of friendly exchange; or, in other words, the way to 'succeed' in the context of the fraternity is to become proficient at receiving and at initiating acts that embody mutual recognition and thus mutual honour or respect. Honour itself is not here the heavily charged privilege of aristocracy that it so often is in pre-modern societies, but a kind of contracted dignity, an agreement to speak the same language and listen to the other as an equal. And in this as in other ways, Bossy's 'charity' is very like a *game*.

Games are unproductive. The point is not to make anything concrete out of the common activities agreed, but to perform the activities themselves. And while games may be competitive, the reward of competition is in the first place simply recognition as an exemplary performer (games can be won without prizes being awarded). There is certainly an element of this kind of competition in the behaviour of mediaeval fraternities or those involved in pre-modern festivals; but what needs to be emphasised is that this is not competition for limited goods, so that what one gains another loses. Since social activity outside the framework of 'charity' *is* regularly characterised by the sense of rivalry for limited goods, the festival or the

[7] Bossy, *Christianity in the West*, p. 59.

fraternity comes to be a vastly important redefinition of what is involved in acquiring 'goods' at all. The material world appears as a world of scarcity – at least in the sense that no material acquisitions can be infinitely divided out. The game of 'charity' is based on the implied proposal that there are goods to be worked for that are completely different in kind from material goods, goods that exist *only in* the game, within the agreed structures of unproductive action.

We can easily overlook just how eccentric a proposal this may be. David Lodge's barbed novel of academic manners, *Changing Places*, depicts the dim English hero, Philip Swallow, trying to introduce his American hosts to a parlour game called 'Humiliation'. 'The essence of the matter', one of the Americans later reports,

> is that each person names a book which he hasn't read but assumes the others have read, and scores a point for every person who has read it. Get it? Well, Howard Ringbaum didn't. You know Howard, he has a pathological urge to succeed and a pathological fear of being thought uncultured, and this game set his two obsessions at war with each other.[8]

Manifestly a good game: the 'goods' to be won in the game are very precisely at odds with the kind of competition prevalent in the general environment. When the obnoxious Ringbaum finally gets the point, he practically ruins his academic prospects by admitting he has never read *Hamlet* (a problem for a professor of English). But this is a very extreme case, serving only to point up what is subversive about games in their 'pure' form. And the fact that organised sport has now become a major 'industry', with performers competing for colossal cash rewards (and

[8] David Lodge, *Changing Places* (London, 1975), p. 135.

the corruption that goes with that) is an oblique testimony to this subversive and potentially baffling element. Games, we seem to assume, are too important to leave to players, who might perform for pleasure. And the kind of politician eager to promote competitive games as a form of training for competitive economic activity, or what have you, has missed the point with impressive completeness; or perhaps has *got* the point, that games left to themselves dangerously mock and relativise other sorts of competition.

Charity is bound up with the spirit of carnival, in the sense that it challenges any assumption that we are, as human beings, committed first and foremost to victory in the battle for material goods. There is such a thing as a social good (a social miracle), accessible only by the suspension of rivalry and the equalising of honour or status. Nothing is to be won for possession – as in the simplest kind of game, where winning is immediately dissolved by starting the game all over again. Thus the 'ordinary' activity of achieving or acquiring status is shadowed by activities in which status is *assumed*, mutually granted, as a condition of play: not everything depends on competitive performance. Something is seen as prior. We could say that charity here also has to do with *conversation* – an activity that need not be productive, that presupposes mutual recognition, an activity in which 'success' is measured simply by the maintenance of the activity itself. Charity becomes visible where it is clear that certain bonds are treated as already established, not as always *to be* established; where it is assumed that the basic human position is not that of individuals uneasily making treaties with each other, but of exchanges of recognition, acknowledgements that within or alongside or against the world of calculated cooperation – and calculated non-cooperation – is a realm where the possibility and reality of exchange and common concern are agreed or given beforehand. At the most basic level, no one *decides* to start talking. In a crucially important sense, language is not an *invention*, a way of solving a problem. The very idea of a problem to be solved *assumes* language. This is why it is difficult to theorise about the origins of language and why philosophers have often come to grief trying. The myth that language is something revealed by the divine solves nothing, but it should be possible to see why it is attractive, when the alternative seems to chase its tail so frustratingly.

The forms and customs and relations that Bossy pulls together as manifestations of charity can be seen as celebrations of this sense of something prior to negotiation. But the paradox is in the entailment that these voluntary associations and designer rituals are supposed to recover or maintain contact with those aspects of the human situation that aren't chosen or designed. On the whole, the bonds or unities we do not choose are linked for us with kinship or nationality; but the trouble with *that* is that it turns so promptly into an inflated kind of individualism, with its own bloody and bitter competitiveness. But the bonds expressed or recognised in carnival and fraternity are significant because they are not grounded in *anything* contingent or local. In one sense, they are quite arbitrary, even absurd: pure play. But if you treat them as optional, as dependent on any one person's initiative or consent, the game is over. It becomes involved with what it is most supposed to be at odds with – anxieties about power. Why should I follow the rules *they* make? What are *they* trying to get *us* to do? You can't play in those circumstances.

This, incidentally, may throw some light on the difficulties we – typically – get into over the problem of 'exclusive' language, gender-specific terms for human activities seen as privileging male over female. There is a whole range of practices in language that might once have been construed as playful, occasions of charity – religion, metaphor, drama or fiction, and so on. It was claimed that they celebrated common or basic modes of recognition between human beings. But certain kinds of analysis strongly suggest – to put it mildly – that these ways of talking are in fact shaped by a non-playful interest, and encode policies and decisions that both express and reinforce the freedom and initiative of men over against women. We can't, it seems, play any longer. Self-consciousness is always fatal to play, and if we go on trying to play, ignoring the critical analysis, we are accepting as given what has now been redescribed (accurately or not) as the decision of one group against another. Charity has evaporated; or else we have recognised that it was never really there.

This is a problem we shall need to come back to later. What it highlights, though, is the difficulty of carrying on the game of charity if we suspect that it is *really* dependent on someone's or some group's choice. I said earlier that no one decides to start talking, no one decides to start playing, to initiate the non-productive, celebratory subversions that surround the supposedly serious world of material rivalry. We come to the rather bizarre position that these voluntary, arbitrary, groundless activities *cannot* be treated just as ordinary matters of choice: the assumed equality of status cannot simply be withdrawn or conceded by one agent's decision. To play at all is to deny that kind of 'freedom'. Somewhere in and around this awkward acknowledgement lies the shadow of the religious under-pinning once accorded to charity, the interlocking of radical social respect with the honouring of God, the sense that the creation of a fraternity or the invention of a social ritual was not a human assertion or positing of meaning, but an attempt to feel towards and cope with a set of unchosen truths about the universe, and ultimately with the most comprehensive 'fact' of all, the *dependent* condition of the universe and everything in it. The apparent groundlessness of charity conceals a reference to the 'groundedness' of the universe – but in so doing, continues to put into critical or even comic perspective all other imaginable grounds for social cohesion, mutual recognition or allocation of status.

Bossy and Foucault hint at the directions taken as societies drift away from charity; but it is perhaps in the last quarter-century that North Atlantic society has most dramatically shown the effects of this abandonment. Remaining rituals of charity have been more and more eroded. I've mentioned already the translation of sport into industry, surrounded by sponsorship and massive economic investment. But the development of competitive sport (especially football, for some reason) as a vehicle for arbitrary violence between spectators or supporters makes the same point. In a context where what are supposed to be 'ordinary' forms of competition and status acquisition have become charged or problematic, what seems to happen is that play is loaded with the hopes and terrors of non-playful experience. When social and economic competition have become increasingly violent, some will be more systematically disadvantaged, some will become more and more incapable of letting go the compulsive, even exhilarating, struggle for position. Think of the alleged social profile of football hooligans: a certain percentage (probably not a majority) from the long-term unemployed, a further, probably larger, percentage from young or youngish wage earners, doing reasonably well for themselves. The working situation is skewed in two ways. Either there is no possibility of finding a way in to the world of serious economic acquisition and negotiation; or that world takes on an obsessive character – unsurprisingly, considering the bleakness of the alternative. The idea of a rhythm that controls competition by subversive egalitarian rituals becomes more and more inaccessible; sport becomes another tribal engagement. The surrounding environment freights economic activity with so much anxiety that the interruptions of the game seem threatening, not liberating; anxiety and violence are carried over into what is meant to be play.

But this is only to point to a vicious circle. The skewed character of work in our society is intensified all the time by the lack, the thinness or the impotence of the remaining social rituals that embody charity. In such a situation, these surviving practices that point to the social miracle bear too heavy a load, and buckle out of shape, becoming prolongations or displacements of, or compensations for the destructive-competitive activities of non-playful society. Things are not helped by the intensity of media attention: sport, from football to chess, is defined in the media as what – professional – others do. For the professional, there is a need, spoken or unspoken, not only to win within the terms of the game, but also to win in terms of the rewards that publicity can confer, the odd and fragile 'goods' that are supposed to go with celebrity. For the mass audience, this has largely ceased to be *their* ritual: it is something enacted for their entertainment, rather than an activity that might affect their own modes of behaving and of understanding themselves.

Mention of the media prompts a short digression on the rake's progress in perceptions of the British monarchy in recent decades. In a rather curious way, monarchy can act and sometimes has acted as a focus for 'charity', a ceremonial representation of social cohesion, allowing citizens to find at least a form of lateral equality as 'subjects'. This has always sat awkwardly with the facts of monarchical rule: arbitrary patronage (for example, 'the Court' as a locus of unaccountable political power) and attitudes of servility. The tension between monarch as icon and monarch as absolute executive master in, say, Tudor England or Tsarist Russia, is not very easily resolved. But the remnants of sacred eccentricity surrounding the monarch in Britain (touching for the king's evil, presenting Epiphany gifts of gold, frankincense and myrrh in the Chapel Royal or – until the rite was sanitised late in the eighteenth century – washing the feet of the poor on Maundy Thursday) preserved a trace of the idea of the monarch as representative person, whose functions had a good deal of the 'game' about them. The rot set in (from the point of view of charity or play) when monarchs started dressing habitually in military uniform, thus giving an obvious visual and imaginative priority to their role as personifying the state's supposedly legitimate violence. And as this role in turn was rapidly emptied of content, monarchy had to reinvent itself; the monarchies that survived into the twentieth century were generally those most flexible in performing this job. Part of the difficulty, though, lies in the fact that in a basically secular environment there is no easy way back to the model of the monarch as representing the sacred, the unquestionably 'given' in human affairs, the monarch as speaking for a society through the performance of symbolic acts or the receiving of sacral honours. Even the Middle Ages had not been uniformly enthusiastic about such a scheme of things: there were other and better ways of celebrating sacred bonds. It was the erosion of some of these other ways in the sixteenth century that concentrated unprecedented sacredness on monarchy (divine right was no part of the accepted wisdom of the Middle Ages). And – as with football – the concentration overloads and distorts.

What were monarchs to *do* in this colder climate? The answer, certainly in Britain since the high Victorian period, was to become an icon of ordinary secular and familial life: to be publicly what everyone is supposed to be privately. Hence the quite novel interest, from the Victorian era onwards, in the Royal *Family*. Hitherto, the royal kindred had been a confused assortment of higher nobility, interesting (if at all) in the context of court and dynastic intrigue; but now intrigue was to give way to the idea of 'archetypal' family relationships. Royalty do not so much have to do anything special as to undergo publicly the common experiences of their subjects (or mostly their bourgeois subjects). It is no use blaming the mass media here for their obsessive attention to the private lives of royalty (as rather a lot of royal kindred have discovered in recent years). The very *raison d'être* of royalty has come to be seen as the living of ordinary lives in public: the claim to privacy or the recognition of an inner life of stress, unresolved emotion, betrayal or resentment has great poignancy but is in painfully obvious tension with the rationale of royal status in modern Britain. It is true, though, that the methods and expectations of a very sophisticated news media don't help. Tact and collusion once helped to avoid public scandal (think of the astonishing restraint of the British press in the months before the abdication crisis of 1936); but this fitted with a culture of reserve and general expectations of public decency. When the culture changes, the media will want royalty to share in the effects of an erosion of barriers between public and personal; and we end up with the tragicomic situation of an archetypal family publicly experiencing precisely what most families experience in an increasingly exposed way – marital stress, anxiety and depression, confusion about values and purposes. It is a kind of nemesis of the post-Victorian royal myth.

Yet something far more archaic surfaced in 1997 with the death of Princess Diana. The images of her, the images, precisely, that had consolidated her 'iconic' status in the modern sense, often had about them an echo of sacrality – even to the sacredness of the royal touch. Her death produced an utterly unexpected outpouring of 'charity'-related activity, egalitarian rituals to purge unmanageable emotion (whose relation to the actual circumstances of the Princess's death was often pretty remote). The rest of the Royal Family was required to participate in these rituals; remarkably un-modern things were said about the need for the Queen to be present in London with her grieving people, symbolically summing up or giving voice to their sorrow, and so on. It will take a long time to get the measure of all this. It is largely true that the 'performance' of royalty – as has been so often remarked – had become a stylising of our common problems, a soap opera rather than a touchstone of common meanings. Its increasingly demys-tified, prosaic performance, did not stand at any useful distance from us – except at intensified ritual moments, coronations, jubilees, royal weddings. The public enactment of 'ordinary life' fails to jolt us into the recog-nition of bonds and identities that are fundamental and critical, but not exactly ordinary. Yet for reasons that are far from clear, this death occasioned a sort of remystifying. The demand for the 'modernisation' of the monarchy that was thought to arise from these events represents something of a misreading of the signs. The British public indeed showed itself unhappy with royal protocol – but not in the name of a modern and secular ideal (there was little that was remotely *republican* about the reaction); rather what was on view was a potent lament for a lost sacredness, a magical and highly personal, but equally a ritualised, focus for public loyalty. The 'lost icon' was not simply the dead princess; it was a whole mythology of social cohesion around anointed authority and mystery – ambiguous, not very articulate and not easy for either left or right in simple political terms.

II

Some of the locations of residual charity in the 1990s are surprising – not least because of that obviously residual character and because of their socially limited scope. Much of what is said and written about contemporary dance culture, for instance, makes it clear that this functions powerfully as an instrument of charity in the mediaeval sense. Journalists have been eloquent about the 'rave' as a model of un-anxious, unproductive, egalitarian and co-operative behaviour, facilitated by certain soft drugs, particularly Ecstasy. In contrast to other kinds of celebration, we're told, especially those fuelled by alcohol, there is no endemic violence at a rave, and no atmosphere of sexual threat. This may be an implausibly utopian picture, but there is no denying its attractiveness and coherence; and by all accounts the claims about the basically non-violent character of this environment are well grounded. The recent Criminal Justice Act, by imposing panicky and heavy-handed restrictions on such activity, has produced a more active culture of political outrage than we have seen in Britain since the headier days of the poll tax protests – a testimony to the passionate *need* evidently felt for egalitarian, celebratory and non-violent assembly: for institutions of charity.

Unfortunately there are still questions to be asked. This is an environment in which there is a distinctive mixture of (yet again) tribalism (the corporate patriotism of youth) and a quest for anonymity, a cancelling of the particular, including the particularities of the acting self. We are looking at a phenomenon deeply and self-consciously anchored in the separate identity of – mostly – the under-25s, in the musical and social style of one sector of society, largely unattached in terms of family or working commitments. For all its vaunted egalitarianism, it is not easily accessible to those whose social location is different (and there is a faintly paradoxical flavour in the earnest assertion of a civic right to perpetrate large-scale noise pollution). It appeals to the rather un-rooted (not exactly the same as rootless) climate in which the young adult lives, especially in a society where only a minority of under-25s are likely to be in employment with any long-term prospects (if, indeed, they are lucky enough to be in employment at all). It isn't too difficult to see the force of the egalitarian transcendence of the rave culture, and the relative ease with which the ethos is absorbed. To become no one in particular: this is what is offered here, and offered to those who have not yet been able to shape much of an identity in other ways, in the traditional ways represented by early and lasting sexual bonding and early entry into what was once probably a lifetime's job. The structures for organising an old-fashioned identity are remoter, not very attractive, and can hardly fail to look more than ever alien and burdensome. Unemployment and general social fluidity have lifted what once looked like the self-evident pressures to 'settle down': why not extend the latency period, at least for weekends?

It has become quite common for the serious left-wing press to remark on the new politics of the under-25s, shaped by resistance to the Criminal Justice Act, and by a scattering of 'occasional' issues, notably (in Britain between 1994 and 1998) the export of veal calves and the construction of by-passes. There is a significant sense in which this is quite genuinely a politics of 'charity', in which the *style* or medium of action is at least as important as the issues involved, a style that is anti-hierarchical, aimed at short-term effect, passionate, participatory and sometimes anarchically witty. But perhaps we should think back for a moment to some of the issues discussed in the first chapter. Childhood is, amongst other things, a situation in which it is possible to learn how to choose by being protected from an enslaving bondage to choices playfully or experimentally made. Only gradually do loss and risk come into view as concomitants of choosing in the adult world. And the difficulty with a politics of charity is that it so readily ends up as a politics of extended childhood, in which there are no real negotiations to be made. It is as if the muddled erosion of ideas about childhood that I have tried to sketch has prompted this passionate effort to reclaim the space of play whose boundaries have been so consistently violated. But a refusal to learn the language of cost and ambiguity in fact lands you in a worryingly vulnerable position: others will be making decisions in another language, another mode, decisions in which you will have no share; you may be ignored, attacked, humoured, even indulged, but you will not be a participant.

This is certainly not to say that the prevailing forms of political engagement need no challenging; but it is no use, alas, simply saying that these forms are withering away. Issue-based and interest-based politics may often appear to fill the landscape for those involved, but can also mean ignoring the longer rhythms and further reaches of the situations in which issue and interest come to the fore. Thus the egalitarian innocence of dance culture takes for granted a colossal technological hinterland – the production, marketing and reproduction of music, the chemical sophistication required for the development of 'designer drugs', even the Byzantine politics of the fashion industry. How does all this *work*? What makes it possible? Whose labour, in what conditions, whose investment, whose profit? And if the answers to such questions are not completely palatable – as, in a diversified industrial economy, they probably won't be – what sort of changes are possible and how are they to be secured? Again, if we take the issue of the export of live animals in barbarous conditions, the moral dimension looks fairly clear – indeed, it is clear when stated simply in terms of disgustingly cruel practices; but the point at which labour, planning, cost and uncertainty come in is when you ask about the livelihood of a West Wales cattle farmer who is in no position to dictate or control the conditions of the industry he depends on. To say (and this would be a perfectly sensible response) that if a sufficient number of suppliers collaborated in pressing for change something might happen, is a step in the right direction. But it is a step towards the world of long-term strategy, complex economic balances and potentially frustrating negotiations. To refuse this move, though, is to ignore who it is who *concretely* bears the cost of significant decisions.

All this returns us to our central concern. A politics entirely based on 'charity' in the sense of egalitarian transcendence, non-competitive communion, and so on, fails to be a politics at all, because it depends on not recognising the truth that the non-charitable world habitually deals with – conflicts of interest and desire, the unavoidability of loss, the obstinacy of others. It is simply not the case that we are able instantly to recognise and welcome an identity of interest in every other we come across. We are not transparent to each other in that way. We 'learn' each other, we cope with each other, in the trials and errors, the contests and treaties of speech; which takes time, and doesn't quickly or necessarily yield communion.

But here is a clue to understanding some of our confusions about charity. Once again, there is a bit of a vicious circle in evidence: as the institutions and rituals of charity decay, as we lose a common language affirming us where we 'just are', without having to win a place, our political life fragments and corrupts. There are fewer controls on rivalry, fewer qualifications to the picture of social life as essentially or primarily conflictual. And this in turn means that the polarisation, between those who have and those who don't have the means to manage this conflict successfully, intensifies. More people are excluded from negotiating important decisions and are left with no stake in their social environment – and no language about where they unproblematically and non-negotiably belong, no system of charitable symbols. For the losers in the conflict, there is a stark choice between an unrelieved, or practically unrelieved, alienation, and the adoption of some sort of charity-oriented project to take the place of the missing political dimension. The latter is a powerful challenge to a culture of passivity and 'victimage', and the contribution of community politics to the felt welfare of the disadvantaged is enormous. But it will inevitably stand not as a moment in the wider political rhythm but as a radical alternative to 'public' engagement; and this has consequences whose ambivalence has to be acknowledged.

Historically, the point of what Bossy calls charity lies in its complementarity in respect of the negotiating and conflictual world around. Its rationale is bound up with such a context. In one sense, of course, charity celebrates a state that exists supremely in its own right, a state of pure converse on conversation, social joy. But precisely as such, it exists beyond history and beyond what we can know, think or say about civil society and political society. It is 'mythical', though not in the sense of being some kind of pure projection or aspiration. The institution/ritual of charity tells us that to have a language to negotiate or quarrel *in* is already to presuppose the social miracle, the fact of linguistic sharing. Charity uncovers the bedrock of speech: sheer converse, the exchange of sounds in codified patterns and the peculiar exhilaration that attaches just to that. It affirms what it is in language that is 'there' before and after argument and context – which is not self-expression (a meaningless idea outside the frame of converse) but the possibility of recognition.

III

I want to look briefly at the ways in which two very different contemporary writers have dealt with this. Ursula Le Guin, author of a number of brilliant 'alternative world' fantasies, delivered in 1986 at Bryn Mawr College a Commencement Address which has become something of a classic in some circles.[9] It deals with the tension and complementarity between what she calls the 'father tongue' and the 'mother tongue'. This is *not* a distinction between 'how men think' and 'how women think', though the address occasionally veers towards saying something a bit like this; it is meant as a distinction between modes of speech used by both men and women, although the historical and cultural situation of most women means that they are likely to be more at home than men are with the 'mother tongue'.

The 'father tongue', Le Guin suggests, is the discourse of

[9] Ursula Le Guin, *Dancing at the Edge of the World. Thoughts on Words, Women, Places* (London, 1989), pp. 147–60.

power – not necessarily (though frequently) authoritarian or oppressive, but a language designed to get things done, and, with a view to getting things done, to offer 'disinterested' analyses of situations. Thus it is inevitably a language that distances the speaker from what is spoken of; it is most itself when written rather than spoken; it does not expect an answer; 'It goes one way', and it depends on the energy that comes from *fission*, the 'forcing of a gap between Man and World'. It is the language you go to college to learn more fully. 'It isn't anybody's native tongue.'[10]

The 'mother tongue', on the other hand, is 'inaccurate, unclear, coarse, limited, banal ... repetitive ... earthbound, housebound'. It is *essentially* conversational, it always expects an answer. 'It goes two ways, many ways, an exchange, a network.'[11] Le Guin beautifully and memorably catalogues some of the idioms of this dialect:

> Good morning, hello, goodbye, have a nice day, thanks. God damn you to hell you lying cheat. Pass the soy sauce please. Oh shit. Is it grandma's own sweet pretty dear? What am I going to tell her? There there don't cry. Go to sleep now, go to sleep ... Don't go to sleep![12]

This is a language constantly ignored or belittled by speakers of the 'father tongue', regarded as 'primitive'. But without it no one ever learns their real native tongue, the language of transformation, imagination, the conscious *art* (including housekeeping, cooking, making clothes, along with what we designate 'high' art) that makes style, pattern and beauty out of our biological existence. And without

[10] Ibid. pp. 148–9.
[11] Ibid. p. 149.
[12] Ibid. p. 150.

this elusive native tongue, we become incapable of telling the truth, 'telling what time of night it is'. This is very well said, and, as will be obvious, something close to this is at the heart of the argument of this chapter. I suspect, though, that there are some confusions about the distinction of dialects. I'm not convinced, for example, that the 'father tongue' is the sort of utterance that requires or expects no answer. In one sense it clearly does expect answers – responses, arguments, action. And we ought to think about the fact that most of the utterances Le Guin lists as instances of the 'mother tongue' require or expect *no* answer (what's the answer to 'Oh shit' or 'Go to sleep now'?). It's true that written, analytic language cannot be *answered* in the same way as moves in a conversation. But at least some of the discipline of the 'father tongue' is to say things in such a way that someone might be able to reorganise the material or the argument and take it in a different direction. It would be very odd to say of science, philosophy or even theology that they worked without correction, disagreement and exchange, given the actual history of such discourses.

But Le Guin's underlying point can still stand. There is (broadly) purposive talk, designed to change situations in particular ways, and which therefore opens up contests about the sorts of change looked for and who is to execute them; and there is the talk that is *designed* for nothing, that simply articulates a situation, identifies it, we could say, as a *human* situation, one that can be brought to speech. We could put it another way and say that such talk is not dominated by 'interest', by considerations of power and advantage. What matters is not victory but keeping the exchange going. This, I suppose, is the sense in which Le

Guin can say that the mother tongue expects an answer: it is about maintenance, the unobtrusive and hard-to-formalise ways in which people attend to the background regularities of a shared world, and so it values bare continuation, participation in the exchange, in a way that can be baffling or infuriating for someone conditioned to the idea of verbal exchange as an exchange of information or of signals about who's in charge. Death, for example, is surrounded by clichés; many a priest engaged in a bereavement visit will have discovered the extraordinary importance of saying or allowing to be said a whole range of what might look 'objectively' like empty bromides. Some things require saying, and originality is not what's looked for.

This dimension of 'maintenance' is brought out very plainly in the second contemporary discussion I want to refer to. Charles Taylor, the Canadian political philosopher, has published an important essay on the debate in recent political thought between 'liberals' and 'communitarians' – the debate between those who (very broadly) begin with a basic conviction about societies as composed of individuals endowed with intrinsic rights and liberties that require both protection and room for fair and balanced negotiation, and those who see persons as constituted by social and communal belonging and as finding their value or dignity, perhaps even their sense of 'rights', through identification with the values of the community.[13] In his discussion, Taylor stands back a little from these

[13] Charles Taylor, 'Cross-Purposes: The Liberal–Communitarian Debate', in Charles Taylor, *Philosophical Arguments* (Cambridge, Mass./London, 1995), pp. 181–203.
[14] Ibid. p. 189.

questions to ask what it is that differentiates 'matters which are for me and for you, on the one hand, and those which are for us, on the other'.[14] At the simplest level, I may say, over the garden wall, 'Fine weather we're having': my neighbour and I have both been *aware* of the weather, but to begin a conversation about it is to make it something we attend to together. Such conversation is emphatically not just a putative exchange of banal or useless information: the 'information' that I and my neighbour are both enjoying the weather, not very important information anyway, could easily be exchanged or acquired without a conversation at all. But, when we initiate a conversation, something distinctive happens:

> A conversation is not the coordination of actions of different individuals, but a common action in this strong, irreducible sense; it is *our* action. It is of a kind with – to take a more obvious example – the dance of a group or a couple, or the action of two men sawing a log. Opening a conversation is inaugurating a common action. This common action is sustained by little rituals we barely notice, such as the interjections of accord ('uh-huh') with which the nonspeaking partner punctuates the discourse of the speaker, and with rituals that surround and mediate the switch of the 'semantic turn' from one to the other [i.e. how we learn to recognize that another speaker has paused, that it's my turn].[15]

Conversation thus represents, Taylor argues, the break-through into a recognition of common goods, things we *can only* value or enjoy together. He distinguishes carefully between goods that can be, and perhaps need to be, provided collectively (welfare, law enforcement, fire protection and so on), and those that are essentially communal – that is, those cases in which the positive and participatory enjoyment of some other agent is intrinsic to

[15] Ibid. p. 189.

my own awareness of well-being or satisfaction. And this is the foundation for a particular vision of politics, the classical 'republican' model in which citizens participate in ruling; in which government is not always 'them' over against 'us'. 'The bond [of belonging in a society] resembles that of friendship, as Aristotle saw. The citizen is attached to the laws as the repository of his own and others' dignity.'[16]

This is to say, in effect, that the work of politics doesn't get done without a recognition that my good or dignity has no substance, no life, without someone else's good or dignity being involved. This is more than a contract of mutual respect, securing my position by guaranteeing somebody else's. It is an acknowledgement that someone else's welfare is actually *constitutive* of my own, in a way that extends beyond any simple relation between two individuals alone: the ideal position is one in which an indefinite number of agents perceive their welfare as including their relations to each other and their consent to and enjoyment of each other's flourishing. Which takes us back very clearly to the definitions of charity with which this chapter began: charity is about bonds that are not negotiated, not the result of balancing interests. And Taylor is claiming that conversation, friendship, attending a concert with other people or sharing a joke are in fact foundational for any political practice that is not to collapse into an endless bargaining between interests. Such bargaining, Taylor argues, is unlikely to generate 'common sentiment', shared loyalty, because the institutions of

[16] Ibid. p. 191; on 'republican' government, cf. pp. 200–1.
[17] Ibid., for example, p. 201 on the triumph of 'procedural' models of justice, based on 'judicial retrieval'.

government are inevitably seen in such a context as arbitrators, always to be persuaded, cajoled, manipulated or even blackmailed by one interest group or another.[17] Hence the burgeoning of single-issue politics and the decline in the percentage of the US population who actually vote; not a phenomenon peculiar to the other side of the Atlantic, of course.

I've already argued that, in practice, a politics conceived of purely in terms of 'charity' is not really political: it will always tend to ignore (as I think Taylor is sometimes tempted to) the facts of radical inequality and unavoidable contests. A British writer would probably have a lot more to say about the complex relations of *class* with power, and about the struggles to secure access to certain basic goods for the disadvantaged, issues not necessarily helped by the assumption of a classical 'republican' model as a starting point; and a Marxist might observe that Taylor's society sounds impressively untroubled by problems over the control of labour and production or the management of markets. However, I believe Taylor's most significant insight stands, and is entirely congruent with what I suggested earlier. Exchanges of a game-like character, with the 'little rituals we barely notice' that go with them, are the foundation for a politics that looks beyond pure contest and the management of competing interests – that offers a kind of ground for assuming the worthwhileness of the political enterprise itself.

Some of Taylor's critics have seen in the appeal to

[18] An essay by Andy Lamey, 'The Contradiction in Charles Taylor's "Politics of Recognition"', *Times Literary Supplement* 5025 (23 July 1999), pp. 12–15, comments sharply on the somewhat ahistorical features of Taylor's view of distinct cultures and his reluctance to theorise about the complexities of their actual changes and interactions.

'common sentiment' a danger of collusion with racism, or at the very least with static and exclusive forms of nationalism.[18] Taylor is, in fact, careful to identify some of the questions that arise in connection with a strong corporate political commitment to a specific language and cultural identity (Quebec is the example he discusses at length). But it should be possible to spell out why nationalism, let alone racism, is actually at odds with his basic premise. The 'common sentiment' he invokes, like Bossy's 'social miracle', is precisely *not* the celebration of an ethnic identity. Ethnic or national or 'racial' identity is always already something publicly 'there'; which is why there is a difference between carnival or Corpus Christi and a *national* event. The latter will have some things in common with the 'charitable' festival – a suspension of 'normal' rivalries and productive activities – but the unity it invokes is in no sense miraculous. It is a celebration of certain alleged facts about language, history, and (in an often disturbingly loose sense) relations of kinship, facts that are supposed to be there for examination – and are also vulnerable to being revalued in the processes of examination. Supposedly clear ethnic identities are again and again exposed as political creations, usually constructed to support a broader reading of history in the interest of a particular group. This may be a dominant group: Victorian and Edwardian imperialism liked the idea of an 'Anglo-Saxon' identity somehow shaping the destiny of the United Kingdom; myths of 'Nordic' and 'Aryan' distinctiveness had a far more malign and destructive import in the German Reich. Or the story may be told on behalf of a disadvantaged group: national identities, with 'unique' national varieties of genius, were described and defended by the subject communities of the Ottoman and Habsburg empires in nineteenth-century Europe; Wales and Ireland discovered new unities and identities in resistance to English cultural tyranny during the same period. The appeal to a common ethnic identity tries to persuade us to look to some given state of affairs – a common memory, a common speech, a common 'blood' – that will ground shared feelings and overcome tensions. But this given state of affairs, historically speaking, is normally a skilled and selective arrangement of elements that gains its solidity and definition by being deployed against other such arrangements by other groups. 'Common sentiment' is limited in advance by the limits of the common heritage being deployed, one that is ours-and-not-theirs.

I am not trying to dismiss the reality of cultural traditions in their local distinctiveness, nor denying the liberating potential of discovering a shared history or language that has been suppressed or silenced. But we need some strong suspicions in play to avoid turning such a shared experience into a matter of timeless identity or divine vocation or manifest historical destiny. When national identity is invoked in any of these ways, a decisive step is taken *away* from the social miracle. The miracle, the common sentiment, the sense of necessarily social goods bound up with an indefinite number of others, all these surface when we are *not* focussing on the question, 'What do we happen to have in common?' – looking for the answer in some identifiable state of affairs. That can easily become a question about what conditions have to be met before we can legitimately recognise each other as partners. The social miracle, charity, draws attention to recognitions or possibilities of recognition *prior* to any agreement about what we have in common, in history or race, attitude or ideology. Social joy rejoices in the surprise of recognition, not in the establishing of a spuriously objective ground for fellowship outside the present 'miracle' of converse.

To be more precise. If we are licensed to speak to each other, to recognise one another, because of common history or some form of natural kinship, we are saying that there is something beyond the social exchange, some greater, prior, independent reality whose interest and integrity will abide whether or not I actually make human contact now. The social exchange *illustrates* such a common ground, perhaps in some way reinforces it; but it doesn't *constitute* anything in itself. I recognise an other as like me in relation to some third term – the natural feature we have in common, race, class, even opinions. They are 'out there', for both of us. But Taylorian 'common sentiment' as revealed in conversation is different. I discover in the conversations of charity that what we have in common is, in one sense, simply the conversation itself; or rather, that my interest is bound up, not with the 'out there' we may both be referring to, not with the common defence of what we share, but with the continuance of the conversational relationship. And just as the conversation did not need conditions of recognition laid down in advance before it could start, so its continuation does not need assurances of sameness, recognisability, in respect of some external factor. I recognise the other as like me simply in respect of being a speaker and listener in this shared act of conversing; to break off (or to demand credentials) is to refuse the whole process, to opt out of the game, to declare that you are no longer going to recognise;

and of course conversations have such moments, when you realise, with whatever degree of shock, that what you thought was happening isn't – when someone manifestly is not listening or understanding, when you perceive your words being distorted, when you are in one way or another deprived of your conversational standing.

Obviously we are talking about a spectrum of different types of encounter. There *are* conversations stimulated or enabled by a recognition of something 'out there' to which both relate; but we recognise them as non-miraculous, reasonably predictable. There are relations that develop out of shared activity, doing the same thing alongside each other, even though the being alongside isn't intrinsic to the doing; and there are relations that develop in shared activity that is necessarily collaborative, where the along-sideness is part of what is done. Taylor's example of going to a concert in company is nicely balanced between these categories, I suspect; and there are some occasions of shared activity of the first kind that, because of circum-stances, acquire a quality more like the second and third kind. Conversations between mothers in a perinatal unit are 'about' a contingent experience that happens to be shared by the participants; but it often seems to be also a kind of mutual enhancement of that experience *through* the conversation. Personal interest is *felt* as furthered by or through the other, the common experience itself only taking shape in one mind by the sharing of speech; and this might make us reflect on the ways in which the very idea of 'common experience' already presupposes something about language. There are experiences like *performing* in a concert together, a clear example of activity where the 'doing together' is wholly essential to what's done, even though the shape of the doing is externally dictated. And there are, finally, the relations of friendship, erotic partnership or committed life in community, where the conversing relation is itself the heart of the action: what is being done *is* the formation of social joy.

And Taylor's point (and mine) is that a social practice excessively dominated by one or another kind of preoccupation with the 'out there' element in relations lands us in societies trapped by relations of contest or bargaining, relations in which mutual involvement (my interest *involves* yours and yours mine) slips out of view; and these are societies which *as* societies will command diminishing trust and fidelity. The social order appears as a 'something', a mysterious and alien reality that does not succeed in convincing us that it is there *for* us, or that our interests are bound up with its. It is as if the *standard* form of relation between human agents is a temporary agreement by independent partners to do something together, something which could be done by others and done without substantially changing the identity and position of the contracting parties; while in the background is a supposedly neutral system of administration and arbitration that concerns itself with issues wider than an individual or group of individuals can cope with. Because of its role as an arbitrator or tribunal, every particular individual or interest group is likely to regard it as foreign, as needing always to be persuaded about any specific project or local concern.

IV

This picture will not be unfamiliar to those living in

modern Western democracies, especially in Britain and North America. The philosophy of government on both sides of the Atlantic in the 1980s was based on a minimalist picture of the State as a mechanism for getting the sort of things done (war, economic policy) that could not be done by 'lesser' associations, and a strong commitment to 'family values' understood as the expression of kinship bonds and serving as a covert or overt metaphor for patriotic solidarity; nothing much in between was recognised as having any substance. Some commentators in Britain thought it ironic that governments who claimed to be 'rolling back the frontiers of the State' should prove in practice to be responsible for any number of extraordinary interventions in the local and the particular – educational and industrial policy and practice, environmental issues (or rather, often enough, the sidelining of local environmental concerns), even broadcasting decisions. But there is no real contradiction: the State is there precisely as an arbitrator, detached from local concerns; no legitimacy is allowed to local problem-solving, no imagination is invested in the management of conflict at this level, since everything between the State and the kinship group is at best contingent and insignificant and at worst an enemy of individual liberty (that is, the liberty to negotiate strictly on one's own behalf in the social market). Combine this – especially in the USA – with a culture often deeply preoccupied with *rights*, and the fragmentation is even more acute. My position or my interest group's position needs protecting and reinforcing from the tribunals of public order: practical politics thus rapidly becomes a matter of how these tribunals are to be persuaded to acknowledge and enforce claims. It is certainly true that this sort of concern arises from the acute vulnerability of some groups, minority and otherwise disadvantaged groups, in a diverse and increasingly mistrustful environment. But the effect of a policy of arguing claims in this way is ultimately to aggravate both the suspicions that originally prompted the search for protection and the sense that the social order in its public and comprehensive form of legality is essentially something alien.

In our present cultural climate, all this poses an enormous problem. The concentration on rights as the primary focus of political action is a response to the long and appalling history of inequity, the denial to certain groups of a voice of their own, a freedom of self-determination or self-definition. To stand against the pursuit of such freedom is to collude with oppression. The difficulty is that the pursuit of enforceable claims requires me or us, the claimants, to present ourselves as victims, and to quarry our history for suffering in a way that can isolate us further from each other, can even produce the unhappy effect of a kind of competitiveness in suffering ('Our history is more tragic than yours ...'). The macro-political effects of this can be seen in the competing narratives of different groups in the Balkans or central Africa or the Middle East; the micropolitical in the bitter and complex tensions of minority and disadvantaged groups in urban North America (what agenda can be agreed between Afro-Americans, women, Hispanics, gay men, gay women, Asians...?). So much here works against the social miracle; yet there is no simple path to charity by ignoring the imbalance and injustice in our societies that generates such a pattern.

The challenge is to do with imagination: with imagining

relations other than those of master and slave, advantaged and disadvantaged, and imagining a definition of my or our interest and identity that would require the presence and welfare of others with whom I was not forced constantly to struggle for precedence. The liberal project of emancipation and entitlement for those who have been deprived of voice and power, the liberal State's guarantee of positions and freedoms – all this is a matter of means rather than ends. As an end in itself, the liberal State is vacuous: at best it offers a rather inadequate longstop in disputes about human ends conducted by a variety of specific interest groups. Yet in securing *some* possibilities for relations not skewed by concerns about power and advantage, it is an indispensable moment. What then, though? If we could imagine a political system that was more than liberal, it would have to be one that actively supported or promoted forms of social encounter that were not wholly competitive. I suspect that the liberal-versus-communitarian polarisation is not actually very much help here. If the choice were (and *whose* choice exactly would we be talking about, anyway?) between a rights-based order in which particular claims by groups or individuals could be 'fairly' assessed, and a society whose values were established by an unspoken (and unaccountable) community consensus, the options would be unpromising: a 'cold' fragmentation preserved in a rather fragile state of truce or a 'warm' community identity that absolved itself from the difficulties of managing *real* difference and *real* inequality. But there might be more to say if the model we are looking to is what, following Taylor, I've been calling 'conversational'.

Here, then, are two areas for speculation in respect of

the conversational possibilities of a more-than-liberal society: first, how does the state system view the arts? I am not here thinking primarily of state subsidies for high-profile activities that might justify such subsidies by attracting tourist income; nor even of subsidy for experimental and innovative work. These are probably the extremes in contemporary discussion of public funding for the arts – a discussion that, on the one side, assumes the need for simple economic justification for any money spent on creative activities, and, on the other, assumes something like a moral duty on the part of the keepers of public funds to act as (indiscriminate) patrons. What I have in mind is rather the role of public funding in the support of local and collaborative projects in the arts – travelling companies, local youth orchestras, civic museums, 'residency' arrangements for writers in a particular locality, with the understanding that regular readings and discussions are part of the contract – and so on. The subsidising of such activities is a recognition of the arts as activities importantly disconnected from profit-making and importantly linked to the health and vitality of a town or region. Public subsidy entails some expectations of excellence; and this generates skills and sets standards for more informal local ventures. All in all, the message sent is that activities promoting conversation, activities strongly bound up with the notion of collective and collaborative goods, are of significance for the wider polity. They enshrine the charity without which the social world reduces simply to a relentless struggle for advantage; they create situations in which the unlimited advantage of success of one individual or even one sub-group actually undermines the whole activity in question.

Richard Hoggart's recent essay on *The Way We Live Now*[19] has a trenchant section on arts funding, with some solid practical proposals. As he says, 'The arts are to be kept up if we believe they contain works of the creative imagination of which any mature culture should be proud; and, secondarily, if we believe existing audiences could be greatly widened once we gave proper thought to how to set about it.'[20] Hoggart's focus is, rightly enough, the defence of the arts as enlarging the possible ways in which human beings see and speak of themselves, against the profit-obsessions of the new right and the ultimately patronising relativism of a certain sort of fashionable radical. Yes; but we should also, I want to suggest, think of how some of the very *processes* of art as well as its content enlarge the imagination of social belonging by insisting upon patterns of relation drastically different from those that prevail in a context where goods are competed for. And this may in turn suggest, as Hoggart himself intimates, that the ideal situation is one of partnership between public subsidy and voluntary support. If the main or sole source is public money, there are always the dangers, the twin, oppositional dangers, of passivity and complacency and of self-promotion at the expense of others. Some kind of quite strictly matched funding secures the essential connection of the social miracles of art to the public interest of a whole state, while also building into local artistic enterprise the no less collaborative disciplines of self-financing. From both sides,

---

[19] Richard Hoggart, *The Way We Live Now* (London, 1995).
[20] Ibid. p. 233.
[21] Ibid. chapter 10 on sponsorship and its effects.

some of the risks of omnipotent commercial sponsorship, chillingly detailed by Hoggart, are kept at bay.[21]

Second, and reverting unashamedly to the concerns of my first chapter, what messages are given by the educational system about the possibilities of charity? If my arguments here have been right, a good educational institution would be one in which conversation flourished – that is, one where activities were fostered that drew students away from competition as the norm. A good deal of nonsense is talked about competition as the sole guarantor of excellence; anyone who has ever been involved in the intensive work of, say, drama in a school will know something of how excellence is guaranteed by the sense of mutual accountability that characterises such work, rather than by any appeal to instincts of rivalry. To acknowledge someone's distinctive skill and require them to use it in collaboration with a larger project is an important challenge (as well as affirmation) for the individual; and the entire process is part of learning patterns of behaviour that properly pull against assumptions current in other areas of the institution. Some aspects of the educational process are inevitably competitive because *selective* – the examination system being the most obvious case. But there is a dangerous barbarism in encouraging the notion that these aspects are somehow the essence of education. To have pressures pulling vigorously in different directions is a mark of both health and realism in education – at any rate, if 'realism' is defined as having something to do with the variegated realities of social life, as opposed to the realities of the job market alone.

But there's the rub: 'realism' *has* been conscripted into the service of a particular ideology – the notion that education is primarily about refining the skills necessary for an individual to succeed, and, more particularly, to succeed in an environment in which every outcome will be bitterly contested by rivals. For some complicated theological reason, this is now referred to as a 'vocational' emphasis. And, as noted in the first chapter, competitiveness *within* the institution is matched and confirmed by competitiveness *between* institutions. In order to secure a favourable placing in the league tables – in order to become 'competitive' in attracting parental and community investment – a school or college must impress on students their duty to perform 'competitively' and not to waste time. The danger is, or ought to be, clear: the danger of eroding other kinds of learning that occur through particular sorts of *process*.

A brief autobiographical note: I remember with gratitude the experience of a school play in which I took part as a teenager and which gave me, though I couldn't have said so at the time, of course, an abiding benchmark for imagining 'charity'. In a fairly academically intense environment – the Welsh municipal secondary school just before comprehensivisation – it was a salutary surprise to discover the skills – technical, electronic and mechanical – of boys from less academically successful forms in the school; or even the non-correlation between dramatic gifts and the ability to shine in A-Level English classes. Like all such enterprises in schools, it necessarily brought a shift in relations with staff involved in the production: there were the beginnings of the possibility of relating as adult to adult. And so on; a fairly common experience, but, for others as well as myself, I'm sure, a defining moment in seeing the power of something other than bargaining for advantage or running for individual victory.

What kind of priority can any of this have if educational policy is increasingly driven by 'vocational' concerns, in the strange contemporary sense of that word? The more-than-liberal society should be recognisable by a corporately and politically owned commitment to an educational pattern that has room for collaborative creation. And – to pick up a point mentioned earlier in this chapter – it is important to remember that sport, sometimes cried up as a refiner of the competitive spirit, can also and equally be a trainer of the sense of common sentiment and mutual need: paradoxically, the team that plays well in competition is one that has learned to work non-competitively within itself. But perhaps most importantly of all, this whole issue bears painfully on the question of 'moral education', an area heavily populated by muddle and cant at present. Every so often, a public figure complains that children are not being taught the difference between right and wrong; and some other public figure, probably from a certain sector of the educational establishment, will patiently explain that children are being morally educated because they are being given the chance to articulate and discuss how they actually make their decisions. More cannot be expected, apparently, since we lack a clear public moral consensus ('we live in a multi-cultural environment').

Unfortunately, however, this defensive response begs the question. There is in fact a robust cross-cultural consensus on many matters (does anyone expect a British Muslim to argue that there is nothing wrong with rape?); and there is a very clear moral orthodoxy agreed on in the teaching profession (how many educational relativists would accept that the rightness or wrongness of racism was a matter of cultural specificity?). But the most important point is what both critic and apologist fail to see: that moral education is neither the imparting of rules in a vacuum nor the discussion of how young people (think they) decide issues, but is bound up with the roles and responsibilities actually and actively learned in the corporate life of an institution. To borrow a phrase from Amitai Etzioni, moral education involves the attempt 'to *increase the awareness and analysis of the school as a set of experiences*'.[22] It is no use at all to pontificate about the need for 'values' to be communicated if the entire style and pace of an institution allow no room for understanding the experiences of learning in their diversity, or if the institution moves more and more towards a monochrome version of what learning is ('training'); if the institution sees its task as the – increasingly anxious and hurried – job of passing on quantifiable information and measurable skills at the expense of reflection on the character of its common life as educative.

There are plenty more areas in which we could think about the possibilities of charity – institutions, from the public library to the Citizens' Advice Bureau to the credit union or food cooperative, which in various ways represent the more-than-liberal vision and which require some quite complex partnerships between public and private support. But in all of them, the level of *public* investment is an index of how far a society as a whole understands charity,

[22] Amitai Etzioni, *The Spirit of Community. Rights, Responsibilities and the Communitarian Agenda* (London, 1995), p. 104.

how much room it leaves for people to meet and relate as something other than strangers or rivals. Legislation about rights is a worthy attempt to secure social presence for those whose voices have been stifled, but what it cannot achieve is the *felt* recognition of a common humanity granted and welcomed, which is the fruit of events of charity and disciplines of conversation. Equally, of course, it is no use simply appealing to the responsibilities that are supposed to accompany rights; this is where communitarianism of the more naive kind succeeds only in turning upside down the rights-based paradigm, failing to go beyond the question of what we can expect from or claim from each other. No claim, whether we put rights or responsibilities in the driving seat, will make sense without the prior underpinning of recognition. And recognition entails a move beyond the idea that my good, my interest, has a substantial integrity *by itself*: no project is *just* mine, wholly unique to me. I have learned from others how to think and speak my desires; I need to be heard – but that means that I must speak into, not across, the flow of another's thought and speech. And, in all this, in the thinking of what it is for me to think at all, I may gradually understand the sense in which the robust, primitive, individual self, seeking its fortune in a hostile world and fighting off its competitors, is a naive fiction. What lies beyond that understanding is a commitment to the charitable conversation that has in fact always and already included me.

Putting it slightly differently: to recognise the presence and the possibility of the social miracle involves a demythologising, even a dissolution of my picture of what a self looks like – the picture that I am encouraged to think obvious and natural by countless pressures, cultural, political, religious. At the end of the first chapter, I touched on the question of how we might come to the point of seeing our accounts of 'natural' needs and desires as revisable, capable of being *thought*, a point that becomes more and more elusive the more all areas of experience, from childhood on, are colonised by the sovereignty of images to do with marketing and purchasing. In this chapter, I have tried to show how the same question can be raised from a rather different perspective, how it is prompted by the obscuring of the 'social miracle' and the withering or marginalising of conversational models of social existence.

We return to the central problem: how is my 'self' brought into question? It seems that where charity is eroded, so is the freedom to question the self, to challenge the mythology of the atomistic system of desires confronting other such systems. Chickens and eggs, of course: we could not simply say that a decay of critical perspectives on the self *caused* the decay of 'charitable' space in social transactions, nor that the barbarising and trivialising of social experience in the acquisitive-competitive mode *caused* the corruption of our awareness of our selves. But the loss of a questioning appropriation of selfhood and the loss of so many of the institutions of charity go together; one is not going to be restored without the other. With this in mind, the second half of this book turns to look more directly at what has been damaged or abandoned in the way we imagine selves – and in particular the self's relation to its past.

3

Remorse

An internationally celebrated interviewer is engaged in a televised encounter with a recently and comprehensively disgraced politician. Perhaps, the interviewer suggests, the word that the public is waiting to hear is 'sorry'. The politician's response is inarticulate, his face registering a mixture of anger, hurt and bewilderment – as if some finer sensibility had been outraged, as if some crassly insulting remark had been made. Public power – even in disgrace – means never having to say you're sorry.

I have in mind one particular and memorable incident; but the scene and the script have become more and more familiar of late in the North Atlantic world. People are made to pay (after a fashion) for their delinquencies by an active, sophisticated and not very scrupulous news industry; they are occasionally induced to say that they regret 'errors of judgement', or the distress caused to those who trusted them. Sometimes it is possible to shift blame: there is a flourishing market in political memoirs which attempt to deflect reproach on to cabinet colleagues, false friends or open enemies. But meanwhile, destructive and hugely costly lurches in public policy (such as the poll tax in Britain in the 1980s), or cumulative drift, waste and confusion (penal policy in Britain for a couple of decades), or a growing culture of secrecy and non-accountability in some areas of international relations (arms trading, the Iran–Contra scandal of the Reagan administration) continue to characterise the corporate ethos of political life. Whether justly or not, this sense of *unaccountable* behaviour is popularly linked with individual scandals – sexual irregularity, murky financial arrangements ('cash for questions' in the House of Commons). The corporate political culture of the USA is so riddled with corruption in the shape of immense subventions from lobbying commercial interests that it is increasingly hard to recognise any moral authority at all in what is transacted in Washington. In Britain, the defeat of the Conservative administration in the spring of 1997 reflected (among other things) a new level of furious impatience with political secrecy and evasion, sharpened by several scandals or suspected scandals in the mid-1990s, not least the handling of the Scott Report on arms dealing. People want to know, more intensely than they might have done a couple of decades ago, to whom legislators now answer.

The cynical response is that they appear to be answerable first and foremost to the imaginary public created by professional image-managers, the iconographers of the media culture. Failure is failure to sustain a visible style, a particular kind of presence; reversals of policy (over the poll tax; or, on the left, the dramatic flight from commitment to an anti-nuclear stance on the part of party leaders, and the continuing muddle over educational priorities and principles, or the proper role of welfare) have to do with complex assessments of gains and losses in these elusive currencies of style or presence. And a public figure involved in sexual or financial scandal survives just as long as the damage to a collective political image can be contained; sometimes this proves to be a remarkably long period. The recent confusion over President Clinton's sexual delinquencies illustrates a number of complex features in this general picture. His enemies have been perceived, accurately enough, as interested in maximal public humiliation for him rather than any kind of reparation or repentance. Public reaction has been largely dominated by a healthy measure of distaste for this strategy. The President's own public response has been to apologise, as it appears, for the hurt done to his relations with the American people, and a good deal of comment has similarly treated the whole affair in terms of injured relations and consequent trauma as between President and people. Evasion and sentimentality predominate, beautifully instanced in the significant use of the word 'inappropriate' to describe Clinton's lechery. For all the rhetoric of error and appeals for forgiveness, it still seems that the losses that matter are losses to an image with fairly clearly calculable benefits, losses in a market of starkly depersonalised and external goods. To say that one of our major cultural bereavements is *remorse* is to raise the question of whether we are still capable of seeing failure or betrayal as inner and personal wounds, injuries to a person's substance.

I suppose it is not unrelated to what some commentators lament as the loss of a sense of 'honour'. In its most robust form, in pre-modern societies, honour is a category far more solid and deep-rooted than 'reputation' in our own world, with which it might be easily confused. Honour is part of a tight mesh of perceptions and evaluations of what you do, which teaches you what you may think of yourself and expect of yourself, as well as what you may expect of others and they of you. Loss of honour may result from accepting without protest a failure on someone else's part to give you what is owed to you, or from a failure on your own part to conform to what might rightly be expected of you. And such a loss means dropping out of an entire system of exchange, of mutual perception or recognition: nobody knows how to talk to you any longer. There have been, and perhaps there still are, societies where you can die of dishonour, because there is no convention left by which you can go on being intelligibly connected with other people. You cannot reconstruct for yourself what their formalised perceptions and evaluations provided for you. Quite literally, you cannot respect yourself.

Honour has so often been bound up with arbitrary matters – kinship, race, wealth – and has had so many and so obvious paralysing and corrupting effects in societies that it has acquired an unmistakably bad name; we are generally disposed to ignore it as a moral issue. St Teresa of Avila famously castigated the honour-obsessions of sixteenth-century Spanish society, declaring more than once that the sense of honour was the one thing that had to be eradicated thoroughly in the sisters of her communities. She did so, however, on the basis of a detailed model of expectations and evaluations within the Christian community – a counter-system, with sanctions at least as powerful, not so much emptying out the notion of honour as radicalising and broadening it: our honour depends not on contingent social factors, but on our status as the 'kin' of the Son of God.[1]

[1] On this theme in St Teresa, see R. Williams, *Teresa of Avila* (London, 1991).

It is not so easy to ignore the question if we take seriously some of the matters raised in the last chapter. Honour formalises systems of *recognition*, grounds upon which conversation can proceed. More than this, it assumes that the capacity of others to recognise me, to talk to me, is indispensable to how I perceive and experience my self. To lose some dimension of how I am seen and regularly responded to is to lose part of the substance of myself (and all this will be discussed at greater length in the concluding chapter). It is tempting in our environment to misunderstand this dependence on how I am seen as a sign of individual weakness, as if it were always the mark of an unhealthy lack of proper self-regard. But for cultures in which honour is significant, self-regard is learned precisely and only as a way of being-in-society, not as the individual's assertion of an abstract or pre-social identity. This is why in such cultures *shame* is both a personal and a social penalty: it is not just a particularly acute form of embarrassment, which I may brazen out or which I hope will be forgotten, but a real restriction on what I am able to think and feel about myself, as much as on what others think of me, make of me, say to me and understand about me.

A society without even residual traces of honour and shame would be a very odd one. It would have to work on the assumption that what finally secured my identity was, at the end of the day, the exercise of my will, the resources of an individual energy. The constant in my experience would be that I am always able to *choose* to construct a worthwhile picture of my existence; and in this sense I should be invulnerable to that enormous investment of my identity in connectedness with others that is typical of a society oriented towards honour. You might then expect, in a culture without a lively concept of honour, all kinds of difficulty about appealing as a moral sanction to the dangers of diminishing the solidity of the self by ignoring the perceptions of others, since the self's solidity would always be secured by the will's freedom to affirm itself. You might expect a situation in which shame was no longer any kind of regulating factor in what was thought or said about behaviour. There might be a variety of pragmatic replacements for it – the dread of embarrassment, of appearing out of step, the fear of losing public plausibility – but these would have to do with possible disadvantages, weakenings of a negotiating position in the sphere of public transactions, not with possible moral injury to the self. You would expect an immense investment of energy in strengthening the image of the willing or choosing subject, whether by a therapeutic rhetoric of 'feeling strong' in the face of adverse circumstances, or by a market environment encouraging ideas of free-floating consumer liberty and offering a range of *styles* as an aid to a creative will. You would, in short, expect an environment rather like ours in the contemporary North Atlantic world.

A confidential tape is released on which a politician can be heard arranging to cover his tracks after conniving at a criminal action designed to blacken his opponent's name. Another politician ardently denies on a Monday his involvement in a sexual or financial scandal, calculating very exactly the level of evidence likely to be available and the level of support for which he can rely on his colleagues; on Wednesday, after a new item of evidence emerges, or after his colleagues have made their own calculations about PR damage, he resigns, subsequently admitting mistakes but complaining bitterly of the malice of the news media and the disloyalty or lukewarmness of colleagues.[2] A prominent executive in a large company resigns when charges of substantial embezzlement are pending; questioned, she explains that her therapist is helping her to feel strong at this time of tension, and to acknowledge how her misdemeanours were in fact a sign of her passive acceptance of the role of a victim or dependant in the organisation. Again, large sections of the quality press are devoted to a painstaking analysis of the subtle distinctions between subcultures in the world of popular music, distinctions involving favoured brands of clothing, drinking habits, dialect. In some quarters, a fascination develops with the phenomenon of the 'cult' book or film, the formation of a small subculture. In the background of all this, though seldom articulated with any clarity, is the promise that the self can be reinvented: in practice, as often as not, this means that identities can be, if not openly purchased in every case, at least selected and constructed from the material that society leaves lying around. Those who have neither the image of a community to shape or make intelligible their choices, nor the purchasing and negotiating power to reconstruct themselves (styles do not come cheap) are left in an alarming state of emptiness in regard to their identity: they are more or less doomed to have identities thrust upon them, identities that simply leave them as objects of mingled fear and derision for those who can operate their choices successfully. Think of the odd process by which the

[2] The pattern became depressingly familiar in the last days of the administration of John Major in Britain in the mid-1990s.

young single mother has acquired the status both of a social threat and of an instance of failure in negotiating power and self-determination; or of the scarifying contempt of the young recreational drug user for the addict. When identities are constrained by this powerlessness in the market, there is not a lot left for the self-asserting will but violence, to others and to oneself in the high-risk atmosphere of hard drugs, petty crime, joy-riding, or whatever.

A culture which tolerates the loss of a sense of damage to the moral identity, the loss of shame or remorse, is bound to be one that dangerously overplays the role of the will in the construction of human persons. Because we live, in fact, in a world where choice is never the imposition of will in a vacuum – as the first chapter of this book attempted to show in a rather different context – a doctrine of the will's power and resourcefulness in constructing and maintaining identities is a doctrine that cannot but distort and obscure a whole range of facts about people's grossly unequal access to the various commodities on offer for building identities, from fashion accessories to professional counselling or analysis. And this means that illusory pictures of our identity are quite directly linked to the springs of violence among those who are dispossessed. It is no use trying to address the self-directed and other-directed violence of much urban poverty without mounting a sustained assault on the most readily available myths about the self in our culture overall. To challenge those myths is itself a necessarily political move, not just a metaphysical observation or an appeal for intellectual conversion.

We *could* say that the problem lay in the lack of an 'inner life'. But that is rather misleading, given the way we so often understand such an expression (again, this will be further discussed in the final chapter). Someone may be powerfully aware of inner images, desires, hopes, may enjoy (or endure) a complex fantasy experience, may even be intrigued, perhaps obsessed, by the analysis of motivation (they may retain a therapist and have a strong concern with 'spirituality'). Such a person could no doubt claim to have a quite well-developed 'inner life'. But all of this would be compatible with a central absence of any vital experience of being involved in or answerable to the perceptions of others; it could easily be a strategy for invulnerability. Interiority can become something appealed to as the locus of an unchallengeable authenticity ('How can I be wrong when I'm so sincere?'). Take away the props, the conditions that allow these styles of supposed self-awareness to flourish and that encourage the picture of a given individual selfhood exploring its constituent elements, and what remains to hold in position a place from which to speak, to become recognisable? An inner life conceived in terms of what I see when I engage in certain kinds of more or less structured introspection is in fact a wholly shadowy affair if it fails to take on board the self's existence in others, the other's investment in my reality. Paradoxically, the inner life as an object for individual scrutiny becomes another externalised production, deeply vulnerable to the contingencies of the material world, the degrees to which the will has access to the mechanisms of comfort and attainment. We need to think through the ways in which the regard, expectation and valuation accorded by another subject deliver a reality that could be more seriously described as 'interior' precisely because it is *not* open in all respects to the simple introspective gaze and not vulnerable to my individual circumstances. It is interior to me not because it is hidden from the other and visible to me, but because it is hidden from *me*.

This needs a lot of further discussion, and the next chapter will attempt some clarification. But the reason for approaching issues about selves and souls by way of reflecting on remorse, honour and shame is that these areas of our human experience and discourse are unintelligible except on the assumption that my past, my publicly identifiable history, the story that can be told of me, does not *belong* exclusively to me. I can set out to reorder it, to rewrite it in various ways, but I don't in fact control it. My actions have had effects and meanings I never foresaw or intended; even the meanings I *did* intend have now become involved with the speech and the story of other lives. I cannot separate out my biography as a thing in itself. But that in turn means that I cannot *absolve* myself; just as I cannot love myself truthfully without another person's love, because I cannot without deceit and corruption love a self abstracted from the vision, involvement and investment of others. If I were able to absolve myself, I should be saying that my acts and their meanings could be – as it were – reclaimed, drawn back out of their life in the lives of others and ordered by my will; and that would be a large and bold claim to a certain kind of power over those others in whom my past is still alive.

The psychopathic killer apparently unmoved by any other agent's perception of his acts is the most obvious example of this enormous energy of self-reclamation; but there are analogies nearer home for all of us. When political regimes change, in Germany in 1945, Romania in

1989, South Africa in 1991–2, it becomes quite hard to find anyone who ever supported or acted for the old order; public figures and administrators reinvent themselves, reclaiming their lives from the lives of their victims in a final and consummate assertion of their power. But the same can be seen in a domestic context. The parent or spouse who has abused other members of a family will, with apparently profound conviction, deny what has been done, or shift the blame on to their victim, thus confirming still further the destructive effects of their actions, the erosion of another person's sense of worth. Therapeutic self-discovery brings to light injuries from formative years; and to begin to be liberated from their effects, it will be necessary to challenge the person responsible to accept the effects – intended or not – of their actions or habits in the past. Refusal of this ('I don't know what you're talking about. You had a happy childhood') risks damaging the processes of healing very deeply, unless the new perception of the self is strongly reinforced by counsellors and friends. We are – painfully – learning more of this as we learn more about the phenomena of child abuse. Yet therapeutically-guided introspection itself is not always innocent. In a society increasingly dominated by the rhetoric of thera-peutic self-discovery, like so much of North American culture, it is possible for therapy to become in turn a tool of denial, a way of neutralising the perspectives of others or retreating into an enclosed frame of reference in which the story of victimisation acts as a total explanation and justi-fication for all the contours of a biography. The agonising and insoluble riddles over the authenticity of some memories of abuse, the questions raised about therapeutic techniques that predetermine what is 'recovered', make this whole area one of the darkest and most complex on the contemporary scene. And, more broadly, there can be a trivialisation of the language of hurt and victimage that serves simply to protect me from the perceptions of anyone who might be my own victim. I am allowed to think as if my presence in the life of someone else is a matter for which I now have no active responsibility; my involvement with others in the past becomes first and foremost something done *to* me, a relation in which I do not have a primarily active role. How are we to find our way to a therapy that recognises *mutual* presence, effect, investment, in a situation where therapy is so often prostituted in the service of creating or restoring a sense of solitary peace with oneself?

II

The denials and refusals of remorse represent a passionate protest against the inexorable conclusion that my past is not under my control. For all that we tend to think of the future as the unknown and uncontrollable, the fact is that the past is just as bad, or worse. George Steiner's story, 'Return No More'[3] outlines a particularly harrowing encounter, at several levels, with the terror of an uncontrollable past, owned by too many contesting minds. Werner Falk is a German, returning to the village in Normandy where he was billeted as a soldier at the time of the Allied landings. He was responsible for the execution of a son of the family with whom he was

---

[3] George Steiner, *The Deeps of the Sea and Other Fiction* (London, 1996), pp. 149–96.

lodged, but he has come back to court and marry the younger daughter. He attempts in two ways to soften the shock of his return: by describing the nightmare he endured himself in his home town of Hamburg during its fire-bombing, when he was made to shoot a woman in terminal and intolerable pain from phosphorus burns – a woman who was in fact, he believes, his sister; and by appealing to the fact that only in the nondescript quiet of the Norman village did he ever escape the shrill violence and unremitting tension with which he grew up in the Germany of the Reich. He is trying as best he can to accept his responsibility, agreeing that the 'grave' he emerged from in the peace of the Norman farm was all too promptly filled by the farmer's executed son, and that there is no reparation possible. Yet he is also looking for a language to share: he too has been hurt, literally crippled, by the continuing machinery of violence and reprisal, and now longs for some way of turning the whole history towards the light. Arguing passionately with the woman he wants to marry, he insists that renewal and reconciliation are not the simple, the trivial options.

' . . . On the contrary. It's much simpler to stiffen in silence or hate. Hate keeps warm. That's child's play. It would have been much simpler for me to die in Hamburg near the canal . . . Do you think it's easy to come back here? In Germany we don't talk about the past. We all have amnesia or perhaps someone put an iron collar around our necks so that we can't look back. That's one way of doing it. Then there's the other, the unrelenting way. Steep yourself in the remembered horrors. Build them around you like a high safe wall. Is that any less easy or dishonest?'

She lashed out 'God knows I wish the past didn't exist! I didn't ask for these memories, did I? You forced them down our throats . . . And now you come and tell us we should forget and live for the future. You're spitting on graves.'[4]

He protests: he is not asking anyone to forget, but pleading for remembrance of *all* the war's victims. ' "If you think of all the dead, of yours and of ours, it will become more bearable." '[5] Movement has to begin again; something purposive must be done.

The marriage is agreed. On the evening after the ceremony, Falk is kicked to death by youths from the local farms, including Blaise, the youngest of the family he has become so bound to. Has he simply come back too soon, as the old farmer mutters at the end of the story? Yes, but the force of this powerfully unsentimental fiction lies deeper. There will be *no* proper time for return, because Falk's narrative of redemption, resurrection, is not his alone to tell: one man's empty grave is filled by someone else, and that death in turn sets off its own consequential stories. No one, it seems, is free to develop their own personal story of healing, because a thousand small filaments unite them to those they have touched, even those they have touched indirectly. Is Falk making an illicit, an impossible claim? In one sense, yes; but he is doing so with a full, articulate awareness of the need both to acknowledge the dead and to find a common language, grounded in shared injuries to the soul's substance that are beyond reparation or explanation. If there could be a path to redemption, surely this is it.

But there is no alchemy that can be relied upon; whatever is *said*, the past remains, violently, itself, a foreign

[4] Ibid. p. 176.
[5] Ibid.

country indeed. Steiner leaves us with insoluble tensions. There is no hope without remorse – the return to the victim, the acknowledgement of what is beyond mending or recompense, the proffering of one's own pain and unfreedom not as a weapon but as a gateway into talking together (into charity?); the alternatives are as Falk depicts them, hatred or amnesia. But acknowledgement and the will to charity can guarantee nothing. Remorse is not automatically a lever to change things, least of all the past.

What Steiner points us to is the uncomfortable *powerlessness* of remorse. To acknowledge the past, the past in which I am enmeshed with countless others and which I cannot alter by my will, is entirely and unavoidably a risk, an exposure of vulnerability. When it meets hostility, refusal to understand or inability to understand, it has no sure solutions; the new conflict that may be generated will increase the sense of helpless involvement in the lives and agendas of others. Remorse, in other words, doesn't bring history to a standstill. What it offers is something quite other, and not by any means so attractive: the possibility of *thinking* history, living consciously in time. Refusing remorse is refusing to think what it is to be a subject changing according to processes and interactions outside my will: to take refuge in the mythology of the invulnerable core of free selfhood, always equipped to construct a desired identity, is effectively to say that the roots of my identity are not in time. As hinted earlier, this mythology can work in more than one way. The idea of an actively free self selecting what it is to be, is complemented by the self-as-victim, a 'true' identity overlaid by things that happen to it, but capable of being excavated and reconstructed, free of the accidental deposits of a personal history.

Remorse involves thinking and imagining my identity through the ways in which I have become part of the self-representation of others, groups or individuals; and so learning to see my (or our) present style of self-representation as open to question. It is in some degree to make *internal* to myself what I have been in the eyes of another. At the corporate level, this is, of course, a highly charged matter. If the former colonial power makes reparations to the indigenous peoples of its old territories, it will look like a confession of weakness or uncertainty about its role and standing. It will be an admission that its own account of its past is vulnerable to revision in response to what others perceive and say. It will impinge on the lives of a large community, whose sense of their worth and identity may be bound in with a particular version of their nation's past, a version in which the perception of that country by others has never played any part. The anger and dislocation this can generate has been much discussed in Britain in the last couple of decades, as the imperial account of Britain's history has been increasingly discredited and displaced in the educational system. But the process is in many ways made harder by the rhetoric that surrounds the whole question of reparation: understandably, more is demanded than bald acknowledgement; but, in emphasising the claim of the victim and the right to press for something like a restoration of the *status quo ante*, it risks its own denials of history and involvement, risks refusing a future that is actually *different* precisely because of the complex of injurious but undeniable relations that are now part of a colonised people's past. Once again, we have to do with the question of identities in *time* and the seductions of anything that looks like offering an escape from them. And a related point has to be made about the mindset of the former imperial or colonial power: no language about this is helpful or truthful that simply expects from the present-day community an acknowledgement of past crimes in terms of simple present guilt. Such ways of talking end by cheapening the currency of the language of remorse and responsibility.

But this does not alter what is most fundamentally required, which is the relinquishing of an identity placed beyond challenge or judgement, and the moving into a sense of identity that admits not simple guilt but the manifold ways in which we are real in the language and narrative of others rather than in a privately scripted and controlled story. This admission is unavoidably and painfully a loss of power; but what I have been suggesting here is that to try and conserve power in such a context is to lose moral substance and to refuse the work of historical thought. Putting it slightly differently, you could say that remorse has to do with finding the self in the other; refusing remorse amounts to defining 'real' selfhood out of both time and conversation. And such a refusal stops me understanding that what I now am has been *made*: that is, it is not fixed or obvious, not the result of a neutral, natural process, but is the deposit of choices, accidents and risks. If I am not capable of understanding this, I shall see myself as a bundle of 'natural' phenomena – instincts, desires, affinities – not open to critique, not capable of being thought through or articulated in recognisable speech. In political terms, this is the seedbed of fascism and violent xenophobia.

The 'timeless' self is, of course, much the same as the consuming self we looked at in the first chapter – the self

making choices without loss and without inner consequences. Change occurs for such a self not through the
slow and difficult processes of learning new ways of seeing
and speaking my history, new modes of productive labour
in our speech and imagination, directed towards that
history which is necessarily not the possession of one
subject; change is conceived either as a simple assertion of
will or a capitulation to the will of another – as if change
were never anything but violence. But this is also what
makes for such a morally thin atmosphere in the discourse
of rights touched on in the second chapter. It is worth
pausing further on this tough and contentious issue. As
noted earlier, to challenge the language of rights is to risk
colluding with ignorance and oppression: our talking
about rights has taken shape as a way of affirming what it
is about human beings that cannot be negotiated away or
extinguished by the claims of sectional interest. The
problem arises with the possible implication that what is
non-negotiable or 'essential' in human existence is
primarily a set of abstract entitlements; which in turn
suggests that actual historical conditions are secondary to
the imperatives of meeting a cluster of timeless conditions.
It is then possible to assess and condemn any specific
complex of historical relations according to their failure to
embody the entitlements laid down in some kind of
primordial charter for human life. What comes *first*, it
seems, is a self to which certain things are due.

But this sounds dangerously mythological if we are
learning at all to think of selves as being formed in
particular histories, particular kinds of interrelations. And
if there are no primitive individuals possessed of entitlements that can in some way be enforced in the tribunals of

public life, this does not mean that we are stuck without any ground or impetus for questioning what happens to prevail in any given social or political order, that we have no reason for challenging patriarchy, racism or whatever. The point is how we construe the 'essential', the aspects of human history deemed not to be vulnerable to the disasters of political history. Talking about human beings in the context of conversational relation takes it for granted that human subjects are *difficult*, complex, that understanding calls for time; if forms of relation prevail in which this difficulty is denied and other subjects are constantly being drawn into one party's agenda and definitions, there is – manifestly – no conversation in any significant sense. In consequence, no *thinking* is going on: the processes of power are still working at a pre-reflective level and neither party in the relation is engaged in specifically human activity. In plainer English, oppression is a situation where people don't talk to each other; where people don't find each other difficult. One party's language reaches out to incorporate the other's experience, which cannot speak for itself. The white supremacist who sincerely claims to understand what the black population 'really' wants; the male (psychiatrist? theologian? novelist?) who meditates uninterrupted on the essence of femininity; the fashionably radical historian passing judgement on the ethics and ideology of an earlier culture; the 'Orientalist' discussing Asian history, or the secularist discussing the Middle Ages – all these represent not an infringement of 'rights' but a failure to begin thinking, a failure to find things difficult in the characteristic way human language implies that they are difficult.

This is relevant to the concerns of this chapter because

different pictures of what is 'basic' to human subjects produce different models of what is possible and appropriate in relation to the complex question of guilt and injury. If we begin from the individual with claims, an injury will be seen as an infringement of these entitlements, the abiding loss of something like moral property. To rectify the situation, someone (not necessarily the original offender) has to recognise this loss and determine what might make it good. What is in view is *reparation* – which could involve the literal restoration of property (as with aboriginal land claims in Australia or Canada, a matter of much bitter public contention), with, in its train, very often, counter-claims about infringements of existing *de facto* title. When slaves are emancipated, slave-owners demand compensation; twenty-odd years of feminism, and men begin to complain of their disempowerment. What this model does *not* deliver is a sense of historical violence or dispossession as a breakdown in the possibilities of speech and thought, a failure of human self-representation in talk and in common life (in charity): something that decisively injures and changes the offender as well as the offended. The loss in question is not moral property but moral *presence* as enacted in a true conversational relation. But if we are starting from this point, what 'makes good' loss or injury will not be simply the enforcement of a claim and the restoration of property, but the creation of some possibility of speaking together, or thinking one's own reality through the medium of another's history, seeing oneself in the other.

The language of right and claim, when it becomes the dominant form of moral discourse in a society, may well be a factor in muting the possibility of remorse in the fullest sense. In such a context, recognising responsibility for the condition of a victim is to recognise liability, a potential rival claim to goods that are currently mine. I am threatened with loss; and there is inevitably a strong incentive to resist admitting to anything that would expose me to the adverse award of a tribunal. The victim is a *competitor*. But, in the perspective of convictions about interrelation and language as fundamental, remorse is the recognition of a loss already experienced by myself and the other; and the victim is a *partner* in the labour of restoring thinking and converse. What is 'due' to the victim is the freedom to share in the definition of who and what they are, to participate in the exchange of conversational presence. This is an always unfinished task, because (as was suggested earlier) each fresh moment carries its own possibilities of misstatement and misrecognition of self and other. But in risking such misapprehension (and the risk, as in Steiner's story, may be a great deal more than theoretical or verbal) the language of remorse at least avoids the stand-off that the language of rights seems to be condemned to; it does not wait for the restoration of a situation in which all entitlements are satisfied before engaging in social converse, challenge and even cooperation. *Civic* life, public argument and contest and negotiation about what might be practical and desirable goods for everyone in the manageable short term, requires the impatient and risky engagement of partners in what may be still a very imperfectly equal field. Odd as it may sound, there is a way of talking about rights that stifles this vital civic process and debate by its appeal to a kind of abstract, suprahistorical tribunal to settle the matter of reparations before any positive social future can be thought about. What tribunal could equalise the score of deaths in Northern Ireland, let alone Rwanda? What could count here as a satisfactory settling of offences or payment of debts?

There is, of course, a very fine line between this invocation of the need for civic vitality rather than abstract settlement of claims and a potentially corrupt appeal to social cohesion as an imperative that overrides the protests of a minority voice. But it may be quite important simply to recognise that there *is* such a line. The distinction between a society of vocal and sometimes quarrelsome citizens and a society of claimants arguing rival bids before a tribunal is a perfectly real one. What is essential in preventing the corruption I have spoken of is a certain scepticism about appeals to 'social cohesion', a recognition that social unity is not ever something unproblematically given or achieved. What I've called civic vitality actually assumes that such cohesion is always in formation: its shape is not yet given and could not be present in any sense without the release, the becoming-audible, of all potential civic voices. What we have to try and separate in our minds is, on the one hand, the emergence of a civic voice engaged in public debate about shared goods and the emergence of a *plaintiff's* voice, requiring satisfaction. In a society more and more preoccupied with this latter model, where being a victim is almost the essence of being a moral presence, one of the hardest tasks we face is the transition from acknowledging inequity and injury to active common labour and language.

And one of the things that makes this particularly hard is the implicit demand for victims to lose their innocence. As claimant or plaintiff, the oppressed, silenced self is simply a sign of another's guilt; the morally interesting business lies in dealing with *that*. But as an acknowledged 'civic' voice, as participant in the defining of goods, the self emerges into risk. As an agent involved with others, it lives with the possibilities of new misapprehensions and exclusions; in the terms of this book's first chapter, it becomes involved in adult choices. To settle for being primarily or essentially a victim is to say that my identity is not something for which or in which I *labour*, to treat identity as buried and static. 'Labour' entails the risks of staking my selfhood in ways vulnerable to change and to critique.

In short, the relation between oppressor/aggressor and victim, in a context where remorse is not properly available, leaves *both* in a strikingly similar position. There is a competition for moral security, for the ability to bear your own scrutiny with confidence. Aggressors can maintain security because they do not allow any other perspectives into the images that define the self except those that are securely controlled: the idea that some portion of moral substance is invested in the uncontrolled histories and discourses of others is something to be ignored or resisted. And the victim is secure as a self that has not yet been required to act, a self whose status has been determined by the acts of others; at best it is asking for the possibility of action and self-determination, at worst it is bound to the role of passive innocent, perhaps intensifying it by the refusal of anything less than total reparation – which is always inaccessible, since our history cannot simply be either unravelled or halted. Two kinds of timeless identity; two selves attempting to stand outside language and difficulty.

III

It is not too hard to put flesh on these abstractions; we have only to look at the aftermath of pretty well any major reversal or upheaval in power relations in recent history. The white South African is emerging from a culture that is – intriguingly – shaped *both* by the denials of the oppressor and the pleas of the victim. Until recently, the dominant culture of the white population was pervaded by the refusal to admit that its moral substance was in any way affected or injured by the massive structural inequity prevailing in the country. It was not unknown for defenders of the system to claim that the old Republic of South Africa approximated closely to a truly 'Athenian' democracy, a civic enterprise of egalitarian converse; though such defenders did not always note the fact that might confirm the parallel most closely and uncomfortably, the fact that both depended upon a slave economy. Within the white population, Afrikaners in particular (though not exclusively) refused to think their identity *through* thinking their relations with the non-white population – refused, therefore, to think what it was to be *African*, to be where they in fact were. The life of the township or he 'homeland' might be deplorably deprived, and the conscientious white person might give time and resources to lessening such deprivation; but it remained quite strictly immaterial to the self-perception of the dominant culture (deprivation being put down, perhaps, to the sad congenital incompetence of the 'African', or to unfortunate but in principle transitory economic contingencies). At the same time, this self-perception on the part of Afrikanerdom was significantly shaped by its own history of victimage – the 'desert wanderings' of the Great Trek, fighting off hostile tribal attacks, the struggle with the British Empire, the period of suffering and brutal discrimination at the hands of the British (concentration camps, the attempts to curtail the Afrikaans language). The internal and external battle against apartheid in the last few decades has been in significant part a battle against this deep-rooted and deeply felt myth of innocence; it has been far more than a straightforward struggle for shared political power or equitable land ownership. It has been a demand for the relinquishing of a particular kind of moral self-image – and has undoubtedly been experienced by Afrikaners precisely in these terms.

The world being the way it is, moves towards power-sharing in South Africa were prompted by pragmatic considerations as much as anything. The maintenance of white privilege by 'freezing' the great majority of the total population within the constraints of a low-wage, labour-intensive economy becomes harder and harder in a competitive, market-oriented international situation. However reluctantly, the dominant population has to begin to see its economic interest as bound up with factors in the international market beyond its control and definition. The early days of Nationalist government in South Africa were marked by a curious kind of idealism: the country might be doomed to economic stagnation, but it would be fulfilling its God-given task, wholly misunderstood by the world around, of pastoral and patriarchal care for an inferior race. This ascetic vision was effectively dead by the end of the fifties; but the implications of operating in a modern international economy took time to sink in. By the mid-eighties, the tensions were widely acknowledged within South Africa to be unsustainable. And the limited but persistent nuisance of international sanctions played some part in this process as well. But it cannot then be surprising when political change turns out to be less than straightforward; self-perceptions don't necessarily alter when economic and political constraints do. The new dispositions of power will be in many respects costly to the formerly dominant group, and this will, for some, reinforce the myth of victimage, even where this does not take the overtly pathological forms of militarised Afrikaner nationalism. Not all the tact and imagination of a Mandela can avoid this.

And this means that all kinds of troubling questions about the past are left unresolved. If a significant proportion of the white population remains privately wedded to the self-perceptions that reinforced apartheid, even when the structures have begun to shift, what real political conversation, what 'charity', can emerge between former masters and former slaves? How far can the native African trust the former masters, now that their behaviour is – perforce – different? Is the past really named and dealt with? Because if it isn't, the prospects for common 'civility' are poor; as noted earlier, such refusals to confront the past deny the passage of time and the reality of vulnerability. This can result in a further turn of the screw in the self-perception of the oppressed: I sense that I am seen (or half-seen) in much the same terms as before; only now this has become structurally less visible, it is also harder to call to account. Frustration threatens. And there is also the tension in the post-revolutionary situation arising from the dual need somehow to bring the guilty to judgement and to build the civic institutions that will cement mutual trust and help to dissolve the easy and fixed roles of oppressor and victim. It is a tension much in evidence in the workings of the Commission for Truth and Reconciliation presided over by Bishop Tutu. The establishing of the Commission was a genuine attempt to deal with the problem of naming the past without falling into the trap of insisting on legal reparation or retribution – an attempt at a massive exercise in national therapy, bringing recent history into a more honest focus. Its difficulties are painfully obvious. The Afrikaner and European communities have shown only a very limited willingness to review the stories they tell of themselves, and such confessions as have been forthcoming have often been felt to be less than completely serious precisely because they cost little in terms of public shame, let alone punishment. The good intentions of the Commission have appeared at times as having the effect of cheapening the very language of truth and reconciliation. What is more, a further shadow appeared in the 1997 hearings, over Winnie Mandela's activities. Memories of township violence are in any case easily invoked by many in the white population to show how all-pervasive evil was in the eighties (we, the white population, are not the only villains): if we are disputing the moral high ground, what about the casual and senseless butcheries of township gangs? Was Mrs Mandela indeed responsible for a reign of terror, and how far does collusion with such terror extend? The past, in other words, might be troubling to an ANC loyalist as well as to a supporter of the Nationalist Party, because it questions the innocence of the oppressed; just as the new situation, in which the ANC activist now has the responsibility for meeting or failing to meet the demands of the African population at large, is fraught with the risk of guilt and fresh division.

Thinking about South Africa in such terms does not, emphatically, mean that its situation is worse or more hopeless than elsewhere. Quite the contrary; it is just because South Africa has managed so radical a transformation with so little public violence in the immediate process, and because its new administration has shown itself capable of such moral seriousness (as reflected in the Commission's work), and because it has been characterised by extraordinary levels of public generosity and patience from former victims of oppression that it focusses so clearly the problems that remain. Even in a situation where the practical risks of serious and large-scale violence seem to have been contained, and where there is willingness to move beyond recrimination and the demand for reparation, the fears and tensions over the possibility of remorse are still immensely powerful; it remains a threat to any safe possession of a moral self-image. And my argument so far in this chapter suggests that the international culture of which the new South Africa is becoming a part will do little to resolve such anxieties. South Africa should remind us that the corporate selves of dominant and oppressed groups in a society do not simply lose their histories by the fact of structural change; they thus remain vulnerable, tense and mistrustful constructions to the extent that these histories are not thought and imagined afresh.

More painfully, we might look at the moral tangles around the state of Israel and its relations with its neighbours and minority populations. In the background, there is what is still the major moral and political trauma and outrage of the twentieth century, the attempted extermination of a community identified not only as dispensable from the point of view of a dominant group, but as positively *requiring* to be exterminated, dispensed with, for the 'health' of the wider society. How are we to think or speak about a situation that goes so far beyond the relatively simple matters of oppression or master–slave relationships? It is not possible to consider Jewish responses to the Shoah as just a very extreme version of the 'plaintiff's voice'. Again and again, the literature moves towards one or another kind of silence; beyond protest or even claim. And this in turn leaves other communities – the ones that failed to see or intervene or identify at the time of the genocide – with nothing to say. Perhaps this is actually beyond remorse in the ordinary sense: the injury to the 'moral substance' is just too deep for retrieval.

That is what we might hear in some of the passionate rhetoric of the Israeli Right: if no remorse is possible or effective, if nothing can be said that changes or moves on from the memory of outrage, the relation of Israel (understood as the moral heir of the European Jewish history of this century, and all that led up to it) to what is not Israel is unlike other political relations. Israel always remains the martyr community, facing the possibility of diabolical assault and destruction; what Israel does will always be a defence and a protest against this unchanging fact. Hence the situation in which Israel is seen by some of its vocal citizens as never involved in *merely* political negotiation, never being a political community among others in a region. We are invited into a frame of reference beyond politics, almost beyond history. The Holocaust silences some kinds of discourse, some kinds of poetics or theology

– a well-worn theme in European and North American philosophy and cultural theory in the last few decades; but it also, paradoxically, establishes an incomparably radical new beginning for the settler communities in Israel, the remnant. Here is a territory of promise restored, a surface on which new meanings may be inscribed, free from any guilt or complexity attaching to the centuries of exile. For such a community, the issues around remorse, the finding of the self in the other and the painful forging of a shared world that comes out of this, are not readily accessible or intelligible.

The non-Jew can only observe from an embarrassed distance, carrying the weight of post-Holocaust silence. But the observations can be voiced, if only because so many Jewish thinkers have voiced related anxieties about what can become a solipsistic and apocalyptic vision of a world beyond politics, time and guilt. There are those, like the late Gillian Rose, who press the question back to the sources of such an apocalyptic vision: will it do, finally, to treat the Shoah as beyond *thinking*? In a brief essay on 'The Future of Auschwitz',[6] Rose challenges the two most obvious reactions that might be evoked at the site of the death camp – an identification 'in infinite pain with the victims' on the one hand, and, on the other, a tormented questioning as to whether *I* could have done this. Instead, she proposes, the question that needs to be evoked is, 'How easily could I have allowed this to be carried out?'[7] This question, according to Rose, focusses the central tragedy of the modern consciousness. Beyond

[6] Gillian Rose, *Judaism and Modernity. Philosophical Essays* (Oxford, 1993), pp. 33–6.

[7] Ibid. pp. 35–6.

the simple oppositions of innocence and guilt, victim and torturer, lies the overwhelming fact of modern politics, the militarisation and mystification of the state as an impersonal mechanism. This represents a schism between my moral awareness, my scrutiny of myself as (more or less) self-determining, self-forming, agent, and my political location as a subject involved in processes beyond my control, processes for which I can disclaim responsibility.[8]

If I understand Rose at all correctly here, she is intimating that the Holocaust is 'beyond remorse' not because it is a diabolical evil that resists analysis, or an apocalyptic break in habitual historical interaction, but because it shows how the modern alienation between public and private goodness, law and morality, can leave us with no vocabulary for thinking and speaking about evil, guilt or tragic loss in the public, political sphere. Faced with such things, we don't know who is responsible, and are (guiltily) inclined to feel a little relieved; it can't be pinned on *us*, even if we adopt the fashionable language of corporate guilt and corporate apology.

In this most extreme outrage, the paralysis of 'ordinary' notions of remorse, the apparent impossibility of reparation and the exaltation of the martyr community to a place outside 'ordinary' politics in fact brings into sharp relief the basic problems of remorse as experienced in personal matters. Failure in remorse is failure to find ourselves in the other; in the context of the modern atrophy of political morality, it means the failure to recognise the moral loss to us as agents that results from

[8] Ibid. p. 36; cf. several other essays in this collection, notably 'Of Derrida's Spirit', pp. 65–87, and 'Walter Benjamin – Out of the Sources of Modern Judaism', pp. 175–210.

the corruption and untruthfulness and barbarity of corporate life. If we cannot even begin to think the memory of the Holocaust in relation to the language of remorse, we cannot properly identify the reality of *political* evil – which leaves us with the unhappy gulf Rose speaks of between the self as moral agent and the self as political or civic subject. To put the Holocaust outside what can be thought about is to set in stone the division between what conscious reflective agents do and what mysterious collectivities do. The savage debates over whether it is right to attribute the genocide to more or less innate historical tendencies in the culture of Germany, whether the average German was virtually predestined to be a 'willing executioner', are not helped by a certain failure, on both sides, to consider the nature of strictly political evil, the dispositions of power and responsibility that might concretely allow Germans or anyone else for that matter to become, collectively, executioners. And the use to which the militarist Israeli Right can put the mythical and apocalyptic model of the Shoah as a unique break in language and history should give us some pause. It reinforces, by the bitterest of paradoxes, the precise problem about the relation of morality and law that produces our own (non-Jewish European or North American) moral paralysis on the subject. If the Holocaust somehow takes us beyond language and politics, the actions of the remnant community are outside law and negotiation and the recognition of self in other, and it is no use trying to discuss collective regional security, presuppositions about historical rights of residence on the part of non-Jewish people, politically defensible frontiers or any kindred matters.

126

For Europe, the Holocaust must still be *thought* about: silence, however potent its motivation, can be an evasion here. And thinking about it should direct us precisely towards the ways in which the modern political collective moves us away from categories of shame, responsibility, even the possibility of acknowledged failure in public discourse. This is not at all to domesticate or generalise or reduce the horror of what was done to European Jewry. On the contrary: to begin to think thus is to think of the specific and local human identities extinguished in the slaughter, the identities that belonged already in and with the selfhood of specific others – the specific neighbours and fellow-citizens who colluded, actively or passively, in the outrages of the Reich. A collective and apocalyptic crime against a collective sacrificial victim allows no personal, no local mourning, no political thought (who 'allows' public decision and how?), no sense of the death of charity as the damnation of specific agents incapable of seeing themselves as agents in a public order. This has nothing to do with trying to make the Holocaust bearable or healable, to fit it into a framework where remorse can be uttered and absolution secured. Nothing softens what was said earlier about the risk and powerlessness of remorse; no one can guarantee forgiveness.

But if the very possibility of forgiveness, of some kind of morally different future that moves us away from the relations of torturer and tortured, is not wholly to disappear, remorse has to be 'released': we have to learn to *grieve appropriately*. In another of her essays,[9] Gillian Rose explores the distinction between two kinds of mourning. There is the 'political

---

[9] Ibid. 'Walter Benjamin – Out of the Sources of Modern Judaism', pp. 206ff.

melancholy' which assumes that history is essentially tragic or catastrophic, that the enemies of human welfare are always already victorious. Revolutionary tyranny can rewrite the past: so our present efforts for or witness to justice lie always under the shadow of a possible future cancellation, even annihilation. In this perspective, the temptation is to look for a moment of Messianic or apocalyptic (and therefore violent) transformation, something going beyond the ambiguous and already corrupted process of gradual social change.[10] But, Rose insists, there is another kind of mourning which does not assume despair, and so does not drive us to the longing for violent and magical change. This is what she calls 'inaugurated' mourning,[11] grief that has its origins in the knowledge (in some particular here and now) of concretely possible fulfilments concretely threatened or lost. Such mourning depends upon investing what we perceive with an 'aura', a solidity, a position not ours, from which we may ourselves be seen. And this sense of a specific, located otherness is directly related to 'the ability to know and be known . . ., to look and have one's gaze returned'[12] – and so to the 'acknowledgement of the relation of the other to herself in my relation to myself'.[13] The self-relatedness of what I perceive is its substantiality over against my presence to myself; but that self-relatedness is not a self-enclosure, but the capacity to be seen or recognised, expressed and experienced as a 'look' directed at us, as something that enables our own self-perception. This mutuality is the ground of the ability to sense loss in a particularised way. We grieve because we are aware of loss; but to

[10] Ibid. pp. 206ff.
[11] Ibid. p. 202.
[12] Ibid.
[13] Ibid.

understand loss is also to understand fulfilment or recognition, to have been familiar with 'knowing and being known', and so to be free of despair. There are specific things to be hoped for, which are not cancelled or annihilated because they are bound to the specificity of relations, the concrete differences that are made by one person's selfhood evolving in dependence on others. The mourning that arises in this relational particularity enables me to endure as a 'witness' to other possibilities in the face of catastrophe; even to remain open to the ironic and the humorous; it also, because it recognises that recognition between persons *happens*, allows the possibility and intelligibility of forgiveness.

IV

We are brought back to the central point in this chapter: remorse occurs when there is a sense of the *implication* of my self with the other (the other person, the wider moral or material environment), such that another's loss becomes – not the *same* as mine, but the cause of loss to me, specific, historical loss. If we simply said that someone else's loss 'became' mine, we should be abolishing the distance between me and the other; recognition in the other would collapse into absorption, and we should be left only with melancholy, in which all pain or tragedy is defined in terms of *my* sense of a loss of power or value. As Freud argued, mourning recognises that what is lost is different from the self, while melancholy treats all loss as the loss of something in or about *me*.[14]

[14] Freud's 'Mourning and Melancholia' is to be found in vol. XIV of the standard edition of Freud's works. For an excellent discussion of some of the issues here, see Susannah Radstone, 'Heroes for our Times: Tommy Cooper', *Soundings. A Journal of Politics and Culture*, no. 3 (1996), pp. 191–208, esp. 199–204.

Melancholy is thus alien both to remorse and to forgiveness. But proper mourning *connects* the catastrophe of another with my own fate: it looks towards a potential and lost moment, or a not-fully-discerned level of belonging together, and asks for a new solidarity – which is what forgiveness is meant to create. In a sense, what matters is less the achievement of this solidarity than the asking, because such an asking indicates *hope* and *need* for the lost connection. It makes a firm statement about the human position: that connectedness or recognition is fundamental to any position that can reasonably be called human.

Remorseful mourning does not allow me to be a hero; nor does it allow the fantasy of a new, post-revolutionary order that is 'heroic', beyond the needs expressed in mourning. It bars the way even to the exalted sentimentality of identifying with victims. When Rose describes the two obvious reactions to the Auschwitz exhibitions – identification with the sufferers on the one hand and tortured self-examination on the other – she is describing two kinds of imaginative heroism: the leap of self-abnegating compassion into the abyss of the Other's suffering, and the descent into the dramas of my own will, bravely testing and facing its frailty. She invites us to look away from both, and to see ourselves neither as victims nor as performers or perpetrators, but as suppliants, and as significantly deceived (and self-deceived) participants in a process that is distorting and impoverishing us.[15] A return

---

[15] Rose speaks (*Judaism and Modernity*, p. 36) of 'our sentimentality as modern citizens': ' ... it is the relation between different oppositions – innocence and might, authority and force – between the inner and outer boundaries of our self-identity and lack of self-identity that turns us into strangers to ourselves as moral agents and as social actors'.

to the dramas of the will risks a return to fascism with its massively theorised denials of the really other and its fascination with individual and corporate heroism, the triumph of the will. In relation to the agonies of the political identity of modern Israel, this addresses uncomfortable challenges to both Jew and non-Jew. It questions the apocalyptic isolationism of a consciousness that always assumes the privilege of the victim, just as it questions the romantic inarticulacy of the guilty European consciousness. It requires attention to questions that neither is eager to ask, about what it might mean for Jewish and non-Jewish identity to need each other's interaction or negotiation. It requires – without weakening the empirically exceptional and spiritually nauseating particularity of the murder of the Jews – some language in which the two kinds of grieving involved, for Jew and non-Jew, can speak together.

Rediscovering remorse, then, has a lot to do with the capacity of a culture to leave room for the non-heroic, to celebrate the vulnerable and even the comic. It may sound very strange to associate the sense of the real otherness of a lost object or of another's suffering with the dimension of the comic: but comedy is one very important vehicle for acknowledging and dramatising human involvement in a world that is very imperfectly controlled by human planning, and in which the wills and desires of others frustrate the tyrannies of any single human ego. Comedy typically shows us different kinds of frustration that may be encountered by our planning – the 'hostility' or at least unpredictability of the material environment, and the complexity of different agencies and strategies subverting each other. What makes this comic rather than tragic is that characters *survive*; they are not wounded to death, mortally diminished. Frustration is part of a continuing story, from which people may or may not learn; and the audience is faced with a world in which the failure of control is amenable to being thought and imagined without paralysing terror. The point at which comedy pushes hardest at its boundaries is where such terror is most audaciously evoked. We wonder a little at classifying some of Shakespeare as comedy because he plays so dangerously with terror and loss – Malvolio, Shylock, Angelo ... And perhaps at those boundaries comedy is most powerful, because it doesn't pretend that the risks are small or that the terror is a silly mistake.[16]

But comedy intimates finally that the uncontrollable environment can be the source of deliverance as much as of damnation; if it damns us, as perhaps it does with Shylock and Malvolio, this is, in dramatic terms, because we choose the distinctive hell of placing our own wills at the centre of things (the moral colouring remains incurably ambiguous, not to say offensive, and there is no way of blandly absolving Shakespeare of class and racial cruelty). Comedy is thus deeply inimical to fascism – though it is also deeply inimical to most kinds of planned reform; it enacts a conviction that what finally delivers human welfare or reconciliation is some process supremely indifferent to the images human beings construct of themselves. It isn't an easy idiom, and it is normally a very vulnerable one. Societies in which control and clearly projected images of the self are prized and guarded make

[16] Radstone, 'Heroes for our Times: Tommy Cooper'; see also Mark William Roche, *Tragedy and Comedy. A Systematic Study and a Critique of Hegel* (Albany, NY, 1998), esp. pp. 303–10.

comedy difficult at every level; and what tends to happen is that the comic vision splits between burlesque and satire. By burlesque, I mean simple evocations of the unexpected or embarrassing, episodes of broadly sketched absurdity: banana skins. And by satire, I mean the pointed localised depiction of abuses and self-deceptions, designed to shame or ridicule individual groups, to diminish their public 'honour', with the longer aim of making some sorts of untruthful, self-regarding behaviour more risky and unattractive.

But the very conditions that drive people to satire will also be likely to make satire itself harder and more ineffective. Satire arises when image and reality are ridiculously at odds; but this happens in cultures obsessed with the control and manipulation of images, cultures concerned to lessen the possibility of being properly 'shamed', substantially diminished by losing the regard of others. The whole strategy of public life depends, in such a context, on evading or neutralising or simply rubbishing what might be entailed in the idea of the regard of others. There comes a point where satire tips over into the tragic, where it is an enterprise doomed by its very nature and environment to frustration. Think of Jonathan Swift, the rising spiral of the satirist's fury ending in insanity.

Our century has been well endowed with situations beyond satire. This has, of course, been for diverse reasons. Genocide defies satire, since it is professedly about eliminating the uncontrolled regard of the other. The slaughter of whole communities entails the abandonment of shame. But equally there are varieties of impenetrable bureaucratic cultures that defy satire as effectively because they create and maintain a self-referential and self-justifying dialect. Thomas Merton years ago pointed to the enclosed world of military jargon in the Vietnam War ('To save the village [from the Communists], it became necessary to destroy it').[17] More recently, the records of the Iran–Contra arms deal of the Reagan administration offered an example of the same confident, untroubled, unassailable absurdity and untruth; as did the findings of the Scott Report in Britain in 1996. Both 'Irangate' and the Scott Report prompted satirical versions of the story in the media; but it was hard not to feel that these responses were somehow futile and impotent. The uninhibited British television revue, 'Spitting Image', for once produced a sophisticated and powerful moment, in a programme devoted to the Reagan presidency: after much (often tedious) broad caricature, the Iran–Contra episode was narrated 'straight' by a senior British political figure (David Steel), and introduced by the statement that what followed was impossible to satirise. It is sobering to reflect that this paralysing of satire was achieved not by totalitarianism but by the sophistication of a managerial society, confident in the 'freedom' of its communications media. The irony is that the more tightly and overtly controlled, but less sophisticated totalitarianisms of Eastern Europe produced an extraordinary crop of authentic and humane satirists, from Mikhail Bulgakov to Andrei Sinyavsky or Milan Kundera; rather as if the presence of overt risk stimulated a deeper vein of satirical critique. If you are

[17] Merton's essay on 'War and the Crisis of Language' first appeared in *The Critique of War*, ed. Robert Ginsberg (Chicago, 1969), pp. 99–119, and is reprinted in Thomas Merton, *The Nonviolent Alternative* (New York, 1980), pp. 234–47.

really risking your freedom or even your life as a satirist, you'd better have something worth saying.

One thing that is often noticeable in this sort of satire is that there may be a strong tacit appeal to a common history and (I use the words advisedly) a common myth and iconography. Bulgakov's *The Master and Margarita* blends a folkloric demonology with the poignancies of classical 'realist' Russian fiction and with the evocation of a figure who haunts both Russian folklore and the Russian novel – the powerless Christ, on trial for his life. Sinyavsky's *The Makepeace Experiment* effects a similar blend of traditional themes, retelling the story of the Russian Revolution as a mixture of folklore (the magical and anarchic powers of the 'trickster', familiar from mythologies the world over, the discovery of a magical technique that goes comically and disastrously wrong) and apocalypse (the biblical and post-biblical accounts of the last days and the appearance of Antichrist – a recurrent Russian fascination, found at its most sophisticated in the 'Tale of Antichrist' by the late nineteenth-century poet and metaphysician, Vladimir Soloviev). Satire needs and utilises tradition; you could even say that satire presupposes 'charity', in the sense already defined in these pages, the common points of reference that control individual acquisition and assertion. Eastern European totalitarianism failed to suppress the satirical imagination partly because it was a governmental system imposed upon a largely *pre-modern* base, religious, agrarian, narrative-minded. If satire dies in the 'free' world, one of the incidental casualties of the end of history we hear so much about, this may have a good deal to do with the erosion in Western modernity of this kind of base, of the sense of being located in a significant universe, a folk tradition, a religious metaphysic, even one no longer carrying full intellectual conviction. But that is an issue to which we shall return. All that needs noting for the moment is the difficulty, the frustration, of satire in a cultural environment that successfully manages the images of public life in such a way that it seems as if critical scrutiny is efficiently neutralised in advance, and there are no strongly felt images and narratives to foster scepticism about what is presented and marketed. It isn't that such a culture fully *settles* with the managed images that flood it, or even that it is unaware of what is going on in the processes of management; but the resources and tools are lacking that might change perception and behaviour in the light of other pictures. There is no lively, subversive, taken-for-granted mythology that could shame someone into penitence by displaying them clearly against a generally-accepted or understood moral and imaginative backdrop. Not much is left but burlesque, usually deluding itself that it is really satire.

Some of this is related to that familiar contemporary cliché about the brevity of attention spans in the world of technical modernity. It isn't, in fact, all that reliable a cliché: examples of sustained attention are not too difficult to find (watching a football match requires level of inter-pretative skill, empathy and intelligence that would probably daunt us if they were presented in the abstract). But it does at least register the undoubted truth that the communication systems of the mass media *assume* more and more that interest in and analysis of particular sets of events (a scandal, a war, a famine, a policy decision) are going to be short-lived. The extraordinary phenomenon of day-long news presentations takes it for granted that information means simply the unbroken succession of unrelated complex images. The 'flickering image' of modern media communication, about which so much has been written, represents a very powerful bid to define what really counts as knowledge; and it is a bid that has little room for a sense of location, for irony, for the growth of imaginative under-standing out of a vague hinterland of memories and impressions, or for the sense of a slow unfolding of the consequences of acts and choices. Where events come from and go to is not a question to which the media can afford to spend too much time on, and this helps massively to define how understanding itself is understood – which in turn makes the satirical enterprise harder. In a rapidly-moving stream of images, why should one set of images look more absurd than another?

We are being drawn back towards concerns expressed earlier about time and choice. I spoke of 'flattened landscapes' in our thinking about choice these days, a picture conditioned by seeing selves as if they were timeless desiring and deciding mechanisms; and it is the same seduction of the timeless, the abstract self that is at work in our difficulties over honour and remorse. An abstract self is one that has no life in the lives, speech and percep-tions of concrete others. Once you grant that a self has such a life in the other, it ceases to be timeless, defined by its present self-disposition and self-description. Its *past* is conserved outside itself, beyond its control. And this can, if it is thought through, remind the self of how its options are conditioned or foreclosed in advance by the history of choices made, the inevitable history of loss that makes us actual and not abstract subjects. The controlled self, making its dispositions in a vacuum of supposed consumer freedom and determining the clothing in which it will appear, is a fiction, no less potent for being self-generated.[18]

So what are we to say about a self that is not a fiction, a self formed in time and in relational space, in the uncertainties of language and negotiation about what was once called the soul? All our reflections so far have been, in essence, a prologue to this question. It is one that is easily misunderstood as 'metaphysical', in a rather misleading and malign sense of that much-abused word – a question about invisible essences, the things there might be in the world in addition to the material ones. Talking about the self in such a vein is in danger of being idle and pre-moral. The urgent issue is how we speak truthfully of a material life that includes among its material activities a self-representation that is ventured in the community of other speakers, a material life that somehow *represents* the duration in which it lives. And why this might be territory that is in some respects better charted by using the word 'soul' rather than simply 'self' is the question that our final chapter will try to address.

[18] On remorse, time and the self, several of the essays in Murray Cox (ed.), *Remorse and Reparation* (London, 1999) are enormously illuminating. See esp. Cox's introductory remarks, and the essays by Michael Borgeaud and Caroline Cox, '"The Most Dreadful Sentiment". A Sociological Commentary', pp. 135–44 (esp. pp. 137–8 on the formation of a remorseful self through socialisation), and Nancy Scheper-Hughes, 'Un-doing. Social Suffering and the Politics of Remorse', pp. 145–70 (esp. pp. 156–63 and 168–70 on the experience of the Truth and Reconciliation Commission in South Africa).

4

Lost Souls

A missionary has just returned from years in a remote part of Africa; at the airport in Philadelphia, he is met by his sister-in-law, and they discuss their anxieties (his mother is dangerously ill) as they begin their journey to join the family.

While we were talking in this way, I took the car keys from her, and on the way out of the parking lot I backed into the side of a parked car. It was somebody's brand-new Buick and it was pretty badly dented. I remember jumping out of our car like a jackrabbit. My heart was pounding and I started shouting at my sister-in-law through the closed window of our car. I was screaming something about insurance, calling the police, or whether we should drive away without letting anyone know. I was actually trembling with panic.

My sister-in-law apparently had no idea of the state I suddenly was in; I suppose I was not manifesting it in any gross way ... [S]he was relieved that I took charge in such a calm and attentive way. Fantastic!

The truth was that, inside, I, whoever I was, had disappeared into nothingness. Back in the car, after everything was on the way to being settled and after we were out of the parking lot, the thought of my mother's illness came back to me and also the thoughts of all that had gone on in Africa ...

... But it kept coming back to me in the weeks that followed. At least once a day and then more and more often I would suddenly be stopped in my tracks by the overwhelming experience that my Christianity has

disappeared *because I myself had disappeared!* It was almost always connected
to something minor, some personal irritation ...[1]

The missionary is clear and adamant about the difference
between the loss of self so vividly described here and the
loss of ego that mystics speak of. He has strong 'religious
experiences', he says, in which his sense of identity disappears, but these are comparable to the loss experienced in
the car park after the accident, and leave a similar residue
of bewilderment and self-disgust. They have nothing to do,
as far as he can see, with any entry of the self into selfless
love or any such spiritual ideal. 'I didn't know ... what
secret I had stumbled onto, but no one was going to talk
me into believing it was something good.'[2]

What the 'secret' might be takes time to unscramble, but
it appears to be something like this. Our (North Atlantic)
culture fosters, even in some senses rewards, a privileging
of the reactive over the active in our relations with the
world. We become used to the pressure of stimuli that are
calculatedly and habitually addressed to the more transient
kinds of emotion, hunger for rapid gratification; which also
means that the frustrated emotional hunger, the desire that
meets a shock, an unpredicted check, is overwhelmed with
panic, the sort of panic that shuts out other habitual
considerations as to how I manage my environment. The
American missionary just quoted is describing an early
form of road rage, and his account very reasonably suggests
that the problem is less about traffic than about the inner
life of drivers. But he is also suggesting that *gratified*

---

[1] Jacob Needleman, *Lost Christianity. A Journey of Rediscovery to the Center
of Christian Experience* (New York, 1980), p. 75.
[2] Ibid. p. 77.

emotion in such a general cultural environment is equally an odd and problematic relation to our circumstances, no more healthy or complete than the experience of savage frustration or shock. Whether negatively or positively, what is in focus is myself as absorbing or reacting to a *momentary* and atomised stimulus. What I have called the active element in my coping with my environment is obscured: precisely what *doesn't* come into focus here is the self as initiating, making, transforming. To pick up the language used at the end of the preceding chapter, my responses to my environment do not 'represent' the way in which I exist in time.

This needs a good deal of unpacking, of course. Momentary, reactive relation to the circumstances I am in is in fact shaped by an enormous range of factors, visible and invisible – by a personal history, by various physical constraints, by the ensemble of cultural assumptions that forms my imagination. Nothing is more fatuous here than talk about purely 'natural' desires, instincts or reactions, or talk about the postmodern self's liberty to reinvent itself from moment to moment. What I want now and how I feel now and what I am capable of 'inventing' are grounded in certain basic dispositions, limits and needs in a material constitution; but no one element in this exists without cultural mediation. We learn what we are in language and culture – even what we physically are. What I feel is structured by how I have learned to talk; what I want is what I picture to myself in the images I have learned to form from the observation of others, images that are not innocent representations of objects and goals but complex, differentiated constructions existing in potentially tense relation with the world of other subjects. To isolate the supposed reaction of a moment, to say or imply that any such felt reaction is not amenable to criticism and thought, that it is some *thing* other than the life of a linguistic process, is illusion. To put it provocatively, there is no great gulf between (complex and time-taking) reason and (innocent and instantaneous) passion: there are more and less self-aware ways of talking about passion, more and less in the way of examining how our reactions have been learned, or at the very least, how the representation of our reactions to ourselves has been learned. Thus there is a way of constructing, of talking about or figuring, what's going on that is open to the questions, Why *this* reaction? Where does this sensation or response or desire belong? or, most simply, What's it (literally) *like?* – and is, as a result, capable of representing, however sketchily or inadequately, the time that has made a subject what it is. When there is no such openness, what you have is not an innocent or primitive consciousness but a fictive one – just the same image of a bearer of timeless needs and desires that we looked at so unsympathetically in earlier pages. The point is that it is no less a cultural, language-formed construct than the traditional model of a continuous and reflective self.

But if we live in a culture embarrassed by the inevitability of learning in or through time, suspicious of what seems to be a qualification or restriction of the 'natural' legitimacy of the ego's demands, this fiction will be potent and widespread. Our American missionary was simply documenting the dramatically immediate, barely conscious impact upon him of an environment privileging the reactive, atomised response to situations, an environment generative of a pervasive air of suppressed panic. What is distinctive in his account, however, is his identification of this as a loss of the *self*. I shall come back later to my own reasons for rendering this as a loss of the 'soul'. But it is clear from the missionary's story that part of what is lost is a sense of temporal context: in the reaction of emotional panic, both short-term (his mother's illness) and long-term (African experiences) concerns disappear. Nothing unusual, you may say, in panic reactions blotting out longer-term memories, a wider mental world; but what if our cultural environment increasingly expects, imagines, provides for and nourishes panic? And has no sure means of affirming or restoring the actual 'time of the self', the wider mental world? The missionary's initially puzzling comparison with his 'religious experiences' in the USA seems to indicate that an environment can deliver what feel like highly satisfactory and 'positive' states which are in fact varieties of panic reaction, ways of obliterating a timebound self under intense pressure. It would be interesting, though beyond the scope of this essay, to look into the ways in which 'religious experience' in the North Atlantic cultural milieu is regularly cultivated in such a way as to produce this kind of obliteration, even defined as what successfully delivers a sense of 'timelessness', whether through experiences of 'oceanic' absorption or through varieties of ecstatic states. This is not at all to dismiss the seriousness or significance of such states; but we might need to reflect on what exactly they mean in the broad cultural scene, how they slot into a particular view of what the most desirable conditions for the self might be.

The implication of all this is that the self excluded or occluded in the intense, reactive panic described is necessarily something involved in *narrative*; more specifically in narratives that are constantly being revised, re-edited. If my narrative is simply a cumulative story of things happening, I shall treat each event as an abstract item to be catalogued, and I shall fail to see how what happens reorders what I have been as well as shaping what I shall be. To register an experience *now* is to know that the past I can relate/narrate is now to be seen as capable of bringing me *here*, of producing *these* results; or to acquire a perspective in which the past now appears in this or that kind of analogy, this or that kind of tension, with what's said and done now, and so is changed in some measure (which is why it is not so easy to write dispassionate history, history that carries no implicit comparison with the way we live now). Every 'telling' of myself is a retelling, and the act of telling changes what can be told next time, because it is, precisely, an *act*, with consequences, like other acts, in the world and speech of others. The self lives and moves in, only in, acts of telling – in the time taken to set out and articulate a memory, the time that is a kind of representation (always partial, always skewed) of the time my material and mental life has taken, the time that has brought me here. To step aside from this kind of telling and retelling, this always shifting and growing representation of the past, is in effect to abandon thinking itself or language itself.

The process of 'making' a self by constructing a story that is always being retold is a prosaic and universal one, so much so that we habitually don't notice that it's what we are doing – hence some of the confusions and corruptions this book has attempted to outline. But if we ask what it is that brings us to an awareness of what we're doing, we need to look more closely, I suggest, at two moments that commonly heighten self-consciousness. The first of these is conflict or frustration; the second (which I will examine later) is love.

Now to speak of the experience of frustrated desire as a moment of growth is immediately to invite a moralistic misreading – the idea that conflict is a stimulus to self-development. But more than this is in question here. What Hegel called the unhappy consciousness, the subject aware of its lack of power in making the world intelligible, is not a *stimulus* to development (here's a problem, let me develop my spiritual muscles in overcoming it), but belongs to the essence of development itself. I desire peace, I desire to be at home with myself; but the edge and the energy of the desire, the *movement* involved, comes from the already experienced knowledge that I am 'irretrievably dispersed in a multiplicity of unstable feelings and changing relationships', in the words of a recent and formidably original interpreter of Hegel, Walter Davis.[3] The self I know is the self that is not at one with itself but is moving and changing; the self is always 'in question', under criticism, a matter of thought. This is *implicitly* recognised whenever there is a gap between desire and reality – that is to say, whenever desire comes into the focus of thought, when it is delayed and denied long enough for it to be a problem. It is *explicitly* recognised at moments when that gap is created by a concrete event, a check upon or a refusing of the claim of desire (not just, as in the first instance, when there is an awareness of a process to be gone through before satisfaction can be attained). The

[3] Walter Davis, *Inwardness and Existence. Subjectivity in/and Hegel, Heidegger, Marx and Freud* (Madison, Wisconsin, 1989), p. 98.

more I reflect on this, the more I see that my desire to be (at one with, at peace with) myself is exactly what is frustrated by the very act of thinking truthfully about myself (as an historical and mutable reality); but, on the other hand, the only way in which it is possible for me to be (at one with) myself is to be reconciled to the reality of change and so of frustration – to think through a world where I exist in, and only in, that negotiating with what is not myself spells frustration to a self that is simply looking for identity or self-presence. I can only be where I 'truly' am by recognising that there is no fixed place where I am innocently and timelessly I alone and incorrupt. And the recognition of how I 'negotiate' is what gives me the material for a telling of my self.

'Subject is what it becomes because reflection shows that its being is always at issue.'[4] This particularly dense formulation by Walter Davis means that a self is only really definable *in* the act of self-questioning; reflecting on the self can't be a way of thinking about an 'item' that will stay in focus while we look at it. The act of questioning is the act in which the self is itself. Reflection, says Davis, is 'irreversible';[5] that is, reflection itself becomes the experience that the self thinks about: the questioning of the self, hesitating in its frustration, is the consolidation of selfhood that then, in turn, presents itself for thought. 'Inwardness develops not by escaping or resolving but by deepening *the conflicts that define it.*'[6] To be a conscious subject is to be involved in thinking through what it is to experience check or limit. Which is why (back to our

[4] Ibid. p. 104
[5] Ibid. pp. 104–5.
[6] Ibid. p. 105; my italics.

American missionary) the unthinking, reactive position in regard to such a check or limit is exactly the sign of a loss of self or even of 'subject', in Davis's terms – and the loss too of action, transformation and real linguistic identity. It needs also to be said, though, to avoid another obvious misunderstanding, that this should not be construed so as to deny 'selfhood' to any but the most articulate or self-aware of human subjects. The understanding or thinking of frustrated desire is not primarily a conceptual exercise; it is what goes on (in the child, in the 'handicapped' or senile) whenever reactive emotion gives place to other responses, whenever it is possible to shift into other modes of relating to the situation – not necessarily by what we might want to define as 'reflection', but in whatever still allows acceptance or peace or the taking of a new initiative. Those with experience of the 'handicapped' adult will, as much as any parent, know what it means to discover the resource of the apparently non-reflective in coming to terms with reality.

II

If what has been so far said is true, one of the most powerful enemies of the self will always be anything that encourages us to imagine an environment without friction. George Steiner, in a notoriously provocative essay, suggested that a major part of the difference between European and American fiction lay in the 'Edenic' assumptions of the latter, shaped by a society resolved upon justice, 'a general dignity of mass status', and its concomitant yearning to eliminate what makes for tragic frustration. And in 'Proofs', a novella closely related to the themes of this essay,[7] Steiner sets up a confrontation between an old-style Italian Communist – a skilled proof-reader, literate, ironic and passionate – and a modernising Marxist priest, who argues, with no less passion, that the price of tragedy, difficulty and the art that comes from them is unbearably high. The other replies that, 'Every little step forward is made of sweat and mutiny ... No-one has ever learned or achieved anything worth having without being stretched beyond themselves, till their bones crack. "Easy does it", says America to mankind. But easy has never done it.'[8] Steiner himself admits that this may be massively wrong as an assessment of America (though he is able to point to analyses like that of Philip Rieff – and, one could add, Christopher Lasch – to bear out the diagnosis of a culture obsessed with 'escaping or resolving'); it sits badly with a patient reading of a good deal of the literature of the American South, or even of the mature Saul Bellow. But what Steiner succeeds in doing is at least to alert us to what we might look for, what we might be suspicious about, in the art of our culture (once again, 'North Atlantic' in general terms, not exclusively North American); how we might identify enemies of the self in styles and fictions that erode *difficulty*.

The American missionary we met at the beginning of this chapter is one of a number of figures (some at least semi-fictional) sketched by Joseph Needleman in a rambling and complex but very striking book on *Lost Christianity*, the

[7] The essay is 'The Archives of Eden', included in George Steiner, *No Passion Spent. Essays 1978–1996* (London, 1996), pp. 266–303 ('a general dignity ... ' p. 300). The novella, originally published in 1992, appears in Steiner, *The Deeps of the Sea and Other Fiction* (London, 1996), pp. 313–69.

[8] Steiner, *The Deeps of the Sea*, p. 349.

second part of which is entitled 'The Lost Doctrine of the Soul'. Needleman's theme is that traditional – specifically Christian – doctrine and exhortation are meaningless in our present context so long as we have no idea of what *sense of self* such teaching is addressed to; to hear what is said in religious discourse, we must build a selfhood radically unlike what we take for granted as the modern norm of subjectivity. Hence the apparently throwaway remark quoted earlier about the ersatz loss of self that a modern subject may be able to produce through 'religious experience', as in the case of the returned missionary; religious language and discipline applied or addressed to the modern self produces something importantly different from what the language is originally about. It is this alternative sense of self that Needleman calls the 'soul'; but it is notable that he defines it in terms remarkably close to those used by the secularist Davis writing about the 'subject'. 'The mediating attention of the heart [perhaps parallel to Davis's 'reflection'] is spontaneously activated in man in the state of profound self-questioning, a state that is almost always inaccurately recognised and wrongly valued in everyday experience.'[9] Authentic religious (in this case, Christian) practice begins in the attempt to attend to the moment of self-questioning – to refuse to cover over, evade or explain the pain and shock of whatever brings the self into question, to hold on to the difficulty before the almost inevitable descent into pathos and personal drama begins. 'The soul' is what happens in the process of such attention: 'it is a movement that begins whenever man [*sic*] experiences the psychological pain of contradiction'.[10] But it

[9] Needleman, *Lost Christianity*, p. 167.
[10] Ibid. p. 175.

149

is thus also a very vulnerable reality, since the pain of contra-diction is habitually expected to be eased or removed. The point of bodily discipline, ascetical training, in this perspective is to provide a 'routinised', expected and accepted, experience of contradiction, so that the happening of the soul may build up steadily and consistently.[11]

But in this respect, there is a convergence with some strands of psychoanalytic thinking that insist on the character of the analytical relationship as a place for experiencing a kind of planned frustration. You may begin analysis assuming that what will happen is the learning of truths that already exist but are hidden (never yet brought to consciousness); and this learning is to be facilitated by a skilled professional who is able to give you an authoritative account of what you *really* mean, what is really going on. When 'transference' occurs, when the person being analysed makes a substantial emotional investment in the analyst, this is all about the analyst's position as the person who has something I desire. But the critical importance of working through transference lies in the handling of the frustration, the sense of betrayal, experienced when the analyst refuses to tell me or give me what I want. My perspective, as the person undergoing analysis, is that 'the truth is out there' (to coin a phrase): there is an Other in whom is the secret that will heal me or satisfy me, that will answer to my desire in such a way that I no longer feel the pain of desiring. When the analyst refuses to gratify me, to reveal (or indeed to *become*) the answer to my desire, refuses to put an end to my pain, then and only then may I perhaps begin to understand what a self is and what it

[11] Ibid. chapters 8 and 9, passim.

isn't. Here is an eloquent description from a practitioner, Chris Oakley:

> The encounter that is counted upon is linked to a crucial refusal, that is, the refusal by the analyst to gratify demands of the analysand. Inevitably the analysis begins with suffering ... This suffering will be addressed to the Other, which is where the analyst stands, standing in for the Other ... Eventually the analyst will respond and it is through this that the potentiality in the situation can emerge. This potentiality is for coming up against the realization that the Other does not exist.[12]

If the analysand's desire is met (as, of course, strictly speaking, it can't be, if the theory of the analytical relationship is correct), this would mean that there was indeed a *given* self with specific requirements which could in principle arrive at an immanent balance, identity or fulfilment as and when the requirements are satisfied. Desire would thus become only an accidental feature of the human consciousness. But to understand the pains involved in working past transference, to understand why I *must* be 'betrayed' by the analyst refusing to meet my requirements and aspirations, is what allows me to think my 'self ' as what is coming to birth in the process of experiencing frustrated desire. My wholeness or balance is, ironically, a matter of recognising the fundamental error in the picture of a buried self whose needs can be met once they've been brought to light. Instead, I come to see that I cannot fail to be involved in incompletion; and that *no thing* completes me. My 'health' is in the thinking or sensing of how I am not at one with myself, existing as I do in time (change) and language (exchange). Were it

---

[12] Chris Oakley, 'Otherwise than Integrity', in Robin Cooper, Joseph Friedman and others, *Thresholds Between Philosophy and Psychoanalysis. Papers from the Philadelphia Association* (London, 1989), pp. 120–45, p. 141.

otherwise, the self would not be something that could be thought about at all. It would disappear in the fulfilment of its supposed desire; it would be identical with itself; it would have gone beyond language and reflection. To nurture such a picture while living in a vulnerable and mobile body is a recipe for the most damaging inner dislocations and the gravest dysfunction in relating to a material world in which other perspectives are presented, 'spoken for'.

But Oakley would add that this thinking of myself becomes more and not less accessible if the analyst is able to negotiate the very seductive pressure to become 'necessary' to the analysand. 'One can be lured', writes Oakley, 'into a form of deal, and a great deal will hinge on the outcome of this. If one is engaged in fulfilling the other's desire then paradoxically one deprives the other ... If one allows oneself [as analyst] to be seduced into becoming merely the one who loves the analysand, ... [t]here will have been an abdication from the position of the Other and one will be consigned to being merely an other amongst others.'[13] Thus even the analyst's passion to understand or to heal has to be refused at a certain level if the analyst is not to become simply a presence in the imagination of the analysand, to collapse into the 'sameness' of the analysand's world instead of continuing to stand for a total *difference* that uncovers the incompleteness or fragmentedness of the analysand. And for this, as Oakley hints, the analyst must be persistently aware of his or her own frustrated desire, that desire which is not to be filled up by meeting the desire of the analysand or even

[13] Ibid. p. 142.

by seeking to become (in self-understanding) what the analysand 'secretly' desires – that healing Other who exceeds all desiring.[14] The analyst, in short, can only *represent* the completely Other, the 'non-existent' point beyond desire, when he or she knows they cannot *be* that Other.

The complexities of all this are intimidating. But we might try and summarise like this. The self becomes adult and truthful in being faced with the incurable character of its desire: the world is such that no thing will bestow on the self a rounded and finished identity. Thus there is in reality no self – and no possibility of recognising what one is as a self – without the presence of the other. *But* that other must precisely *be* other – not the fulfilment of what I think I want, the answer to my lack. The therapy that releases or constructs the viable, truthful sense of self that is needed for a life without crippling misperception is a therapy that represents such otherness. And (here is a further twist of paradox) it must represent and not claim to *embody* it; if it slips into the latter, it becomes a new slavery and illusion. The claim to embody the Other says, in effect, that the Other is *here*, an answer, a gratification, a terminus of desire, so that the Other is reduced to the dimension of my lack and ceases to be Other. Thus analyst and analysand must both operate in awareness of the complete absence and difference of the Other, each refusing gratification or completion to the finite other. Each has an interest, as we might say, in the continued life of the other's desire; because as long as that remains radically open, as long as each subject sees and accepts

14 Ibid. pp. 143–5.

incompleteness, each secures the truthful life of the other, blocking 'the illusion of a perfect circularity of desire', the fantasy of a static, symmetrical mutuality of gratification in which the two parties are only 'each other's other', not representations of the liberating Other who does not and cannot appear.

Psychoanalysis understood in these terms (which not all practising analysts would own or even grasp, admittedly) is not just a skilled invitation to the life-giving contradiction or frustration of desire; it works as such by doing something significantly more, by invoking the necessarily absent, non-particular ('non-existent') Other. It is a three-cornered relation, not only a dialogue, in which the presence of the absent third makes possible some kind of liberation from the net of ideas and projections that binds us into the fantasy that some specific other can supplement our lack, once and for all, and end our desire. And the absent, 'non-existent' third is manifest as the condition for a truthful recognition of my own limits, of the persistence of my incompleteness, because it is not itself a point of view, mirroring or competing with mine; it is not another system of desiring, any more than it is something to be fitted into the system of my desiring. Its otherness is radical enough to allow me to be other – to be distinctive, to be the this-and-not-that of temporal particularity. And the finite other who 'holds' this perspective does so only out of the same awareness of the permission given by the 'third' to be a finite self; if this is not so, I remain trapped.

III

I wrote earlier of *two* moments that offer a heightening of truthful self-consciousness. I am stirred into facing what I am as a voice and an agency in time when I encounter what frustrates my unexamined desire, and I can to some extent discover this by discipline, by the classic disciplines of asceticism, certainly – fasting, the contemplative refusal of images, the challenge to hopes for sexual gratification – but also by certain aspects of that odd and ambivalent modern ascesis, the analytic process. But the second moment is less amenable to 'discipline'. In a sense, it is more primitive than what we have just been discussing. It is the experience of being in love.

We'd better be precise: not simply the experience of desiring or being desired, nor an obsessional preoccupation with another, but the moment of acknowledged conviction, shared by two people, that each is accepted, given time and room, treated not as an object of desire alone but as a focus for attention and fascination. In the analytic relation, what prevents the other from dissolving in fantasies of wholeness and gratification are the 'contracted', ritualised refusals of the analyst. In falling in love, what prevents it is a complex of factors – the need to *go on* discovering the other, as well as to have the other as a listening or witnessing presence for my own self-discovery; the almost impersonal gladness that the other exists (especially at early stages of a relationship); the spontaneous (however short-lived) forgetfulness of my own interest, dignity or protection. There is plenty that is paradoxical about all this – and it is formidably easy to sentimentalise. But the truth is clearly that in the relations we designate as 'being in love', the urge for sexual gratification is blended with a range of other affects and concerns that enable the subject to *speak* and see himself or herself afresh. Simultaneously there may be what looks like a naive egotism, the pouring-out of feeling and memory, and an equally naive attention to and absorption in the other's difference and often the other's need.

'A kind of storytelling that makes you coherent is part of falling in love,' says A. S. Byatt towards the end of a long and wholly compelling series of conversations on women writers of fiction with the Brazilian analyst, Ignês Sodré.[15] Both partners in love long to find a way of expressing and discovering truth, because they have been given a kind of *promise*: the possibility opened up by the fact that I am not only physically desirable to another, but someone that another person wants to spend time with, is the possibility that I have a solidity and complexity that demands time to be taken in exploring or uncovering it. The promise is a promise of my being shown to myself in ways I couldn't have realised for or by myself. In the simplest possible terms – I am *interesting*. But how and why is something I can only discover by the twofold process of listening to the other partner (who tells me what I can't tell myself, shows me the face I can't simply look at) and searching for words that will be transparent to what I am, to the reality that I can't see but am now assured is there. Being in love is – familiarly – from one point of view an intensification of the sense of *me*, and from another point of view an intensification of the sense of confrontation with what absolutely is not me. It hovers between egotism and self-denial.

It is a dangerous state and an inherently unstable one. Tilt the balance towards egotism, and the point comes at which I may want to mould or control the interest of the

<hr/>

[15] A. S. Byatt and Ignês Sodré, *Imagining Characters. Six Conversations about Women Writers* (London, 1995), p. 246.

other. Mistrusting the other's capacity to go on being interested or attracted when faced with my mediocrity or my destructiveness, I hold things back, edit and reshape what I say. In other words, I stop discovering, because I am afraid of the open-ended and risky character of what the other is giving me. I must guarantee that this openness does not finally open out on to what in me is unacceptable or frightening. Tilt the balance towards self-denial, and my love may reach the point where I can no longer see myself as solid and complex: my worth is wholly bound up with the other, and my terror is of losing myself if I lose that other. I more and more efface my own agenda, allow myself to be invaded or exploited, offer myself as material for the other's ego to digest, submit to and (consciously or not) invite violence. The two distortions of course have much in common, and at the heart of both is the same dread of loss: loss of the other, at the simplest level, but also loss of the self that the other assures for me – whether I deal with this by reclaiming control over the picture of my self or by unconditionally offering myself to the other's will.

The mutual exposure involved in falling in love is a response to the conviction that there is, fully and unequivocally, 'room' for me in someone else's consciousness and affections. And, as Byatt goes on to say, 'this desire to be wholly contained in another mind, wholly present in a relationship, can be experienced as *dangerously* close'.[16] Sodré agrees that, 'The intense desire for closeness creates claustrophobic anxieties,'[17] and observes how certain fictions derive deep energy from working with the tensions

---

[16] Ibid.
[17] Ibid.

between a longing for closeness, a longing to be possessed or encompassed, and the fear of being so encompassed that my reality slips entirely away from my will and my own proper language. Just as in the analytic relationship, the shadow arises of being *reduced* to what will satisfy another.[18] In shamelessly old-fashioned terminology, we fear becoming objects of 'lust', our significance prescribed by what is acceptable and gratifying. The fact that human beings have historically treated sexual desire as a *cultural* matter – as the subject of social patterning, imaginative transformations, even religious metaphor – reflects something of this fear; which in turn reflects that *excess* involved in what we call being in love, the more-than-desire that enables us to talk about ourselves in a new way. Certainly there is a joy or a confidence that can come from being desired – but only lastingly or securely, perhaps, if the desire opens on to more than the meeting of a need; when it has what a religious person might call a contemplative dimension, a gladness that the other is not 'used up' in gratification. And that is what gives the freedom for telling a story of oneself, even for telling truths that may not seem marketable or palatable.

This in turn (and this is Byatt's point) is vulnerable: to want to be wholly present in another's consciousness can lead to obsessive self-revelation, struggling to leave nothing unsaid, not easily distinguishable from the familiar problem of testing the limits of love by provocative or potentially unacceptable behaviour. The knife-edge is between *freedom* to tell – which allows an other *time* to listen and absorb, and accepts that who or what I am here

---

[18] Cf. Oakley, 'Otherwise than Integrity', p. 142.

will only emerge in this *indefinite* time of speaking and listening – and *compulsion* to tell – I must *now* find the words to deliver myself totally to the other, because if I fail in this I cannot be assured of their love. Erotic love notoriously lives on this knife-edge. When it manages to escape obsession, terror and passionate hunger as its dominant modes, it is because of that space which is more than desire; and this could be characterised as grounded in the knowledge that I can be the cause of joy to another in virtue of something more or other than the capacity to meet their needs.

Which brings us back to the same theme that our reflection on psychoanalysis opened up: to be other, to be distinctive, is more than being *someone else's other*, being what fits into another's stipulated lack. Being in love makes possible 'a kind of storytelling that makes you coherent' to the extent that it realises the odd and elusive recognition of such a dimension. In being very specifically a desired other for someone, I discover that I am more than this; I give not just gratification but joy – which is precisely what isn't planned for, what isn't the scratch for the itch, the demand met. Erotic love, when it is serious and time-taking, when it goes on generating ways of speaking, seems, like the analytical relationship, to move around the non-existent third term: I discover in erotic mutuality the self that is present neither to my own unmediated self-awareness or self-examination *nor* simply to the desiring other. The other apprehends me as not being there – *now*, definitively, finally – for them alone. If you treat the analytical relationship as the provision of saving knowledge to a diseased mind, or if you treat the erotic relationship as a means for assuring relief of tension and a

159

determinate set of satisfactions, what is lost in both cases is that vision of the self as *not* there to be possessed, to be completed or to serve another's completion; the vision of a self that is gratuitous or contingent in respect of any other's need, anyone else's agenda, and that therefore demands time, words and patience.

In other words, what is lost is what I want to call the soul. The religious resonance is deliberate, of course, since what is under discussion is not the 'soul' of early modern philosophy, an immaterial individual substance, but something more complex – a whole way of speaking, of presenting and 'uttering' the self, that presupposes *relation* as the ground that gives the self room to exist, a relation developing in time, a relation with an agency which addresses or summons the self, but is in itself no part of the system of interacting and negotiating speakers in the world. In religious terms, this agency has been seen as the source of the self's life in such a way as to establish that any self's existence is a simple, unnecessary and gratuitous act on the part of the source. The self *is*, not because of need but because of gift. The experiences and encounters we have just been analysing bring to life in us a different kind of selfhood from that of the 'normal' competitive world because they evoke just this sense of a self that is there beyond the sphere of mutual need, and therefore not to be spoken of in terms of the plain self-presence or self-identity of an object. The secular analyst or philosopher will speak of the non-existent or absent or ideal Other (that which is other to all particular others in the world); the religious observer will ask whether such a secular discourse can finally sustain the load placed upon it. The non-existent presence is neither a willed construction nor a theoretical explanation, but a dimension within certain relations that 'shows itself', in the Wittgensteinian phrase. It belongs *within* a discourse about what is made possible in relations between persons, yet does not reduce to an account of transactions between two desiring egos. For any self to be free to enable another's freedom means that it must be in some way aware of the actuality, not only the possibility, of a *regard beyond desire* – and so of its own being as a proper cause of joy, as a gift.

Religious discourses handle this in diverse ways. Northern Buddhism systematically dissolves the whole idea of a substantial self by dissolving the desires and reactions that seem to give it solidity, and then affirms that on the far side of the dissolution is what you might call a paradoxical presence-in-absence for the other that is pure compassion – a love without need because it is without an active centre in the world. The Jewish and Christian traditions take seriously the fact that it is within relations that these insights come to birth, and speak of a personal agency without need or desire shaping finite and temporal agents, agents at whose centre is 'the image of God', the capacity for reflecting God's gratuitous making-possible of the life of what is other – even when this is interwoven inseparably in our lives with appropriation of and action out of a particular position and set of interests in history and society. What these religious perspectives have in common is the conviction that the historical world of negotiation between personal agents with specific interests, while it may challenge fictions about timeless interiority and independence, nonetheless does not in itself deliver the possibilities of a freedom or security for the self that will decisively break through anxiety, rivalry and exploitation. It is only something outside the world of negotiation – as we saw in chapter two – that makes possible the festal abrogation of rivalry, the social miracle. The obstinacy of an other's place or interest is a critical element in understanding what selfhood is in a finite environment; negotiation is the beginning of ethics. But it cannot be its end. The critical possibilities of convergence, equality and reciprocity – the 'ideal speech situation' beloved of some philosophers – requires a recognition of what in us is not negotiable, a common being in time, a common being as gift. And Jewish, Christian and Muslim discourses ground this in the worship of a God who can't be negotiated with, who has no interest to defend and whose creative activity is therefore pure gratuity.

IV

Why has all this become culturally so inaccessible? It is partly to do with the almost infinite corruptibility of religious discourse. Those who claim to speak in the name of God will always be dangerously (exhilaratingly) close to the claim that in their speech, their active presence, the absent God who is never an existent among others is actually present: a claim of stupendous importance in legitimating any bid for power. Here, it says, is a concrete presence that will tell you what you are. The religious ideologue may say – or seem to be saying – that it is as *his* 'other' that you will find your identity (and I do mean 'his', given the history of religious hierarchy in most human cultures); and this will effect a definitive closure on what you are entitled to say about yourself. You are required or desired to satisfy the demands mediated by religious law; that is what you are for, and all you are for.

Now this can be shown to be in various ways a distortion of the underlying logic of much of the Jewish/Christian/Muslim cluster of languages. God is gracious, gratuitous: the creation of a world *unnecessary* to God reminds us that God is not 'needy'; the liberty of God challenges any notion that God can be reduced to a simple or tangible sameness with which we negotiate as we do with the other contingent presences in our mental and physical field. The passage of our speech about God into silence, the self-criticism of all doctrinal utterance in the context of contemplative worship, all this warns consistently against the ideological or hierarchical closures we have just mentioned. But the truth is that such warnings are again and again ineffectual. What the European Enlightenment revolted against was precisely the sense of having your identity and capacity prescribed by a this-worldly other that claimed other-worldly sanction, claimed a kind of identity with the disinterested perspective of God. Enlightenment protested against what seemed the *arbitrariness* of the mediators of the sacred; and it sought to deliver human beings from the slavery of being defined unilaterally by the religious Other *made concrete* in the institutions and conventions of (supposedly) revealed faith. It is one thing to say that we find our identity in relation to or in transparency to an Other outside the systems of need and desire; something else to find that your identity is prescribed, pre-scripted, by the presence and the gaze of an other who is in fact as historical and contingent as you are. It is uncomfortably like the identity of the passive object of desire in pornography; in all the different rhetorics of patriarchy which prohibit a woman's presence to and for herself; in various kinds of racist ideology.

But as the Enlightenment itself collapses under the weight of its own aspirations, it too is seen as potentially a discourse of slavery or pornography, the construction of a normative, rational subject over against sensibility, barbarity, the foreign and the physical. In its origins it had struggled to find ways of articulating what it might be that *every* contingent subject was answerable to. It wasn't first about autonomy in any simple sense but about law – the universally accessible structures and limits (moral and physical) of the world, open to observation, not mediated by the carriers of privately authorised information, power based on revelation. But its own hidden investment in certain sorts of power and enslavement was to be ruthlessly exposed, as the 'universally accessible structures' were dissolved by the various critiques of later modernity. The reasonable environment, visible to all, without mediation or revelation, appeared as a system operating and operated for the benefit of a dominant economic interest (Marxism). The evolution of the knowing subject and his self-positioning in the world of human relations was unmasked as an acting-out of non-rational instincts blindly seeking some kind of equilibrium in a world of essentially material processes (Freudianism). And these acid dissolutions were themselves in turn to be exposed as discourses of a *gendered* (male) subject, defining in advance who is going to count as a speaker worth hearing (feminism – at least as important an intellectual revolution as Freud's or Marx's). Instead of the open space of universal rationality, late modernity has inherited an overcrowded and suspicious territory where every utterance has to be examined, interrogated about the interest it serves, the agenda it (knowingly or unknowingly) encodes and the power it conceals.

Put it more schematically. The Enlightenment objected to traditional authorities on the grounds that they were the products of a contingent history. These authorities had claimed to speak for the Other in relation to which, in dependence upon which, identity was assured and reinforced in a God-directed communal and cosmic order. But if the law and rationality proposed by the Enlightenment as a true and liberating source for identity and order are themselves exposed as contingent, products of particular perspectives and interests, what remains? If law and rationality are only the tools of interest, where is there any space beyond contingency? If *every* other is contingent – that is, if it is what it is by virtue of processes that might have been otherwise – then every other is a rival, a competing interest. And from this point, the self can construe itself in a number of more or less unsatisfactory ways. It can settle for a Romantic or post-Romantic picture of a 'true' self, an 'authentic' core of undetermined will, free to discover and establish its unique moral territory. It can preserve a residue of Enlightenment universalism by seeing itself as a bearer of rights, claims that can somehow be enforced in a tribunal so as to secure a position over other comparable claimants. But both these models, and others that derive from them or reflect them, are fraught with intellectual and imaginative difficulties, some of which this book has tried to trace; they do not allow us to think through what it might be to be alive and concrete only 'in' an other, although just this thought is what our language and experience of being in time constantly invite us towards. But equally, there is a logic of sorts that steps quite beyond any classical images of a unitary self, a narrative consistency making sense of me as a speaker or an agent. The most powerful trends of *post-*modernity argue for the self as a 'site' in or on which the processes of speech, the transactions of power, the sheer mechanics of desire (understood as simple lack) play themselves out. It is interesting, if sobering, to note the current fascination in the arts, especially film and novel, with themes of *addiction* (sexual as well as narcotic): as if there were a conscious focussing on the most extreme figurations of lack, to test what language might emerge and survive in such a context.

Another way, then, of saying what is lost is to see it as the possibility of understanding what it might mean to say that I am because I am *seen* at a certain depth, or that I require a faithful presence to hear my narrative, or that I have no reality as a subject that is not also a reality for and in another subject. If there is no narrative continuity, the significance of the faithful interlocutor or observer disappears. It is worth noting too that all this has a direct relevance to how *bodies* are seen and understood. Systems of bodily convention are the substance of a culture: gestures and practices that regulate eating, sex, even conversation, are assurances that people remain recognisable to each other, that they can in fact speak to each other, that they can be seen and heard. Not to know how to prepare or host a meal, not to know the expectations and limits that make cultural sense of sexual attraction and sexual intimacy, not to be able, as we say, to read signals, not to know how to exchange courtesies – all this is tantamount to a forgetfulness of culture itself. Impatience with what seemed arbitrary conventions, and the characteristic modern conviction that each of us has a hidden self whose authentic expression must be cultivated, have left us with a fair amount of public barbarity and chaos. Particularly in the realm of sexuality, the rapid disappearance of 'codes' has produced not a paradisal erotic liberty but a society more obsessively anxious about sex than most 'pre-modern' ones. Child abuse, professional harrassment, 'date rape' are all marks of a situation in which what we thoughtlessly call 'body language' is actually failing as a structure of communication because we have no *common* sense (and often no common sense) about sex. Not that atrocity, corruption and violence were absent from the sexual life of earlier cultures; but, if my body means what I choose it to mean and your body what *you* choose it to mean, then the fear of a contest between two alien and arbitrary sets of signification in a sexual encounter will be that much higher. Sexual trust, like any other kind of trust, like the social miracle, disappears. It is an extreme case of that typical modern dilemma – being potentially at the mercy of a contingent other who will always be suspected of maintaining their place or interest by violence.

So the body as a site for the will to impose what may be varied and transitory meanings takes over from the body as speaking a recognisable language. It is not particularly surprising that there is increasing interest in 'body art' – tattooing and piercing especially – as another sign of this prevailing understanding of the body; or that some now talk of 'sexual preference' rather than sexual desire. And the cultural anxiety this breeds is not visible only on confusions about sexual boundaries and identities; it runs much deeper. For there remains the passionate desire to *be seen*, to have one's truth not only expressed but somehow acknowledged or validated. Hence the confessional obsession of so much of the mass media, an obsession that has little or nothing to do with remorse or even with the attempt to shape a coherent narrative of movement or growth. What I have to say is the truth of my experience – commonly a bundle of aspirations, recollections and often profound pains as yet un-thought, woven into no connected story, offering little possibility for bridges and exchanges with other narratives. Even a quintessentially modern and liberal commentator like Suzanne Moore, reviewing a clutch of autobiographical books in 1997, could give vent to near-despair at the 'mountains of self-obsession and self-deception that pass for heavily marketed "honesty" these days'. She writes:

> We cannot know or be certain of anything outside ourselves; it is all just too confusing. As the grand narratives shatter into millions of smaller ones, all crying 'me, me, me', myriad voices whisper: 'I may not be a novelist but I know what I'm like'.
>
> ... It is possible to read all this as incredibly liberating, allowing a plurality of voices that have not been heard before. Or it is possible to see it as the symptom of a supreme crisis of confidence in which no one can speak for anyone outside themselves, in which everyone emotes but no one thinks any more.[19]

Our one subject, says Moore, is the subject itself; which means the subject in desperate search of an audience, unable to absolve or heal itself, hungry for therapy, yet, paradoxically (through the medium of the chat show or the uncensored memoir), making itself the object of an undifferentiated alien gaze, making itself the 'other' of anonymous corporate fantasy. There is nothing here of the discipline of absence and frustration, the putting of the self in question, that might make therapy truly therapeutic,

[19] Suzanne Moore, 'How was it for me?', *New Statesman* (15 August 1997), p. 44.

and the problem of the day is *not* that we live in an excessively therapeutically oriented culture but that we haven't a clue what therapy might involve.

The American novelist and essayist, Walker Percy, noted in the early eighties a further symptom of the modern self's hunger and confusion.[20] The autonomous self is lonely: deprived of any means of finding an adequate or satisfying home in the cosmos, it tries to build bridges out of the isolated condition of both human self and human species by demonstrating that we can communicate with other species. 'Why', asks Percy, 'do people in general want to believe that chimps and dolphins and whales can speak, and why do some scientists in particular want so badly to believe that chimps can speak that they will compromise their own science?'[21] We are afraid of being alone in the cosmos as a species just as much as each of us is afraid of being alone with himself or herself. Relating this to what I have been discussing in recent pages, you could say that we are afraid of being left once and for all without an *other* of any kind to engage with. Individually, we find the possibilities of creative exchange and civility, beyond (even if not entirely without) suspicion or rivalry, slipping away from us: there are fewer and fewer conversational others, because of the dominant myths of the authentic hidden self and of the all-pervasiveness of private and competitive interest. But if there were an 'other' for humanity itself, an other *innocent of human history* and therefore outside the human economy of violence, wouldn't we be able to feel assured that we were,

[20] Walker Percy, *Lost in the Cosmos. The Last Self-Help Book* (New York, 1983).
[21] Ibid. p. 168.

after all, the object of a benign gaze, that we were heard and seen as we needed to be?

Such an other might even be sought elsewhere in the cosmos. Percy goes on to observe our interest in the possibilities of communication from extraterrestrial intelligence (not to mention the characteristically contemporary fantasy of abduction by aliens);[22] once again, the underlying agenda seems to be about loneliness. And although the alien intelligence fantasy can be (as so many films and fictions testify) the ultimate competitive threat, it can also hold out the promise of an *innocent* other. It is no accident that the two most popular and most haunting fictions of recent decades about extraterrestrials, *Close Encounters* and *ET*, represent the alien as a kind of holy child. The extraterrestrial intelligence is a voice from outside history, and so seems to offer us a way out from under history's burden; or at least a presence that will define us afresh, give us a place in some wider scheme of things where we are not trapped by what we have done and what has been done to us.

But what if neither whales nor extraterrestrials are going to step in to secure our being-at-home in the universe? Percy is concerned, as well he might be, with the overloading of areas of our human, inner-worldly experience as refuges for what is left of communion and conversation, as means for acquiring a clearer location in the world. In particular, we overload the whole sexual realm – 'the only mode of intercourse by which the self can be certain of its relationship with other selves – by touching and being touched, by giving or receiving pleasure, by penetrating or being penetrated'.[23] Yet this

[22] Ibid. pp. 171–3.
[23] Ibid. pp. 179–80.

enormous loading of significance takes place at a moment when the *meanings* of the sexually engaged body have contracted in an unprecedented way to the limits of individual will and gratification. How then can sexual activity restore a sense of graciously observed presence to a self for whom the body is a surface on which arbitrary messages can be inscribed – not a medium in which or through which a coherent story is built up as part of a language shared by others? Sexual activity separated from promise and acceptance, from ordinary, prosaic fidelity, becomes one more expression of the plight of the self unable to imagine what is involved in developing an integrity over the passage of time. It is the sacrifice of the *body* – as a carrier of shared and social meaning – to the needs of an isolated and abstract subject, reduced to will and need.

These are difficult matters to write about with any plausibility, because the conservative religious establishment, Protestant and Catholic, has tended to react to the simultaneous trivialising and overloading of sex by a rather panic-stricken moralism, for which dissent about styles of sexual behaviour becomes the main, sometimes the only, touchstone of 'orthodoxy' or fidelity to tradition – which is simply to reproduce within the religious sphere the exact distortion and disproportion from which the secular environment suffers. It is little use trying to address this question in isolation from the broader cultural history of the modern subject. But it is within that broader history that Walker Percy sees a further and far more serious problem arising out of our misprisions about sex. In simple terms: when sex doesn't 'deliver', where do we look next?

Violence. 'The demonic spirit of the autonomous self,

171

disappointed in all other sectors of life and in ordinary intercourse with others, is now disappointed even in the erotic, its last and best hope, and so erupts in violence.'[24] Percy is confident that this is likely to be the 'orgiastic' violence of total war; but that may seem marginally less likely now than in 1983, when he was writing (*marginally*). In the 1990s, open communal conflict seems to be the curse of societies other than the technologically sophisticated and sexually liberated. But I suspect that his analysis holds good as far as the violence of the *imagination* goes – as in the steady pushing back of frontiers in what can be acceptably portrayed in film or even in print; and also in relation to the phenomena touched on at the beginning of this chapter, the rise in temperature in public passions. There is an orgiastic quality to the picturings of fictional violence, as there is to some kinds of public rage; and this is to say nothing of the rising tide of domestic violence, *and* the rising tide of rhetorical violence against certain categories of people identified as useful scapegoats – interestingly enough, often groups that are sexually nonconformist, the homosexual, the single mother. A paradox, undoubtedly: but a public in love with trivialised and overloaded sex is quick to turn on those who represent either a costly or even tragic aspect of sexual behaviour. The lone parent, apparently abandoned to the consequences of actions whose results are normally and successfully bracketed, represents an unwelcome note of risk; the homosexual's detachment from prevailing norms represents an uncomfortable relativising of the seriousness of 'ordinary' sex. I really do suspect that some of the

24 Ibid. p. 190.

frenzied anxiety about homosexuality arises less from moral disapproval than from the resentful sense that the homosexual is a kind of mocking *parody* of what most people assume sexual desire to be about. But that is another and a complicated question.

Returning to Walker Percy's analysis, to the idea of violence as the final assertion of a place, of being there, it is clear that this means the end of any possibility of being there *for* the contemplation of some other – since the other's perspective is precisely what is negated in violence. This is what it is to lose the soul, destroying the self by destroying the other. David Mamet's play *Oleanna* was a – grossly misunderstood – attempt to reflect on this in the explosive context of the 'sex wars' of the American campus. John, the male professor in the drama, confronts Carol, a student, confused and intimidated by the whole ethos of the academic institution: his response to her, defensive, patronising, compassionate, all at once, indicates his own confusion (a confusion she has confusedly identified) about the institution he represents. He loves teaching, he claims; yet what we see of his performance and hear of his theory points to an ambiguity – a fascinated love of the *violence* of the institution (whose conventions he has mastered) along with a measure of continuing frustration and bafflement at its pressures, which he too experiences as violent. He is stuck in a Socratic method of dissolution and scepticism without a Socratic vision. John, with his anxieties over status and finance, his incoherently impatient conversations on the phone with his wife and his lawyer (constantly interrupting the supposedly pastoral situation in which he tries to counsel Carol), is a person whose soul is insecurely anchored. He can't help his collusion with all that Carol experiences as debilitating and aggressive.

When she – by a process we don't see and have to guess at – elects to respond to the institution's violence by accusing John of sexual harrassment and demeaning behaviour and language, she constructs her own style of violence, a dramatic distortion of what has happened, to which John's arguably good intentions are wholly irrelevant. Her actions have, by the end of the play, destroyed John's professional life; he explodes in a climacteric moment of real physical threat, but holds back at the last minute. Carol's final words, the conclusion of the play, are brilliantly ambiguous: 'Yes. That's right.' Is she telling John that he has now proved her right? That he has at last acted out openly the abusive and violent agenda of which she has accused him? Or, as she repeats the words, with lowered head, 'to herself ' (so the stage direction instructs), is she acknowledging the truth of his furious attack on her as a 'vicious little bitch'? Is she reverting to her position at the beginning of the play, the assumption of her innate worthlessness?[25]

Whatever the meaning of this ending, each has destroyed the other. The unutterably stupid audiences who applauded (so it's said) as John physically menaces Carol, had wholly missed the ironies already flagged in the opening scene. *Both* are helplessly unformed souls: they enforce their presence to themselves and each other by different kinds of violence; they diminish themselves in their negation of each other, John by his inability to listen to the full range of Carol's distress (and his repeated

[25] David Mamet, *Oleanna* (New York, 1992).

174

distraction with phone calls about his new house, his note-taking while Carol is speaking, and so on), Carol by her deliberate decision to humiliate and punish John by forcing his actions into a pattern that will require official condemnation. They are 'there' for each other only as aggressors. They are souls in hell.

Lost souls: that is ultimately what the 'lost icons' of the title point to. The skills have been lost of being present for and in an other, and what remains is mistrust and violence. It sounds odd, I suspect, to talk of a 'skill' being involved in being present for an other, a 'skill' of being seen; but there is such a thing as a habit of relinquishing controlled self-presentation; or of that attentive stillness which is somehow bound up with *being* attended to. Rilke's famous response to the 'archic statue' – 'There is no place where you go unseen:/You need to change your life' – holds something of this. To be seen: perhaps this is the foundation of any apprehension of the moral self – not, please God, in the sense of being under the all-seeing eye of a judging scrutiny, but the recognition of a life lived beyond the self-referential framework of what *I* choose or understand. This feels like loss and danger. But equally it entails that the resources for my future don't have to be found in or generated by my choice or my understanding. To put it in a deliberately question-begging way, the self that is present to itself and others without violence or anxiety, the self that might possibly be called a soul, exists in the expectation of *grace*. The disciplines touched on earlier in this chapter, the suspensions or deferrals of grati-fication, are, like the experience of erotic love, something to do with the expectation of grace: by deferral, by refusing

175

what *I* conceive myself to want or need, I invite what I don't know, the 'non-existent Other'.

Souls occur when trust of a certain kind occurs, the trust implied in such an invitation of the perpetually absent Other. In the background of much of this book is the question of how our contemporary culture nurtures or fails to nurture trust. Steiner's still problematic and controversial essay on *Real Presences* identifies a deep vein of cultural dysfunction in the breaking of the 'contract' between word and world implicit in later modern and postmodern literary sensibility; and he traces a very direct connection between this and the disintegration of the self. Once words have been 'disinvested' of their involvement with the fabric of the world, the acid of deconstruction leaks into the very notion of the *speaker* of words. 'The ego is no longer itself. More precisely, it is no longer itself to itself, it is no longer available to integration.'[26] What lies 'at the now vacant heart of consciousness' is a chaos of random others – that is, not speaking and relating others, but 'parodistic, nihilistic anti-matter'.[27] The residual self is a site where the traces of what's heard or registered lie around, where unthinking reproduction of received images takes place, where stray forces and chains of causality intersect. It is irreclaimably different from the speaker's self-image as an authorising source or a continuous presence. If there is no presence in words, there is no presence in speakers. If you can't trust the contract between word and world, speech and what it's trying to

---

[26] George Steiner, *Real Presences. Is There Anything In What We Say?* (London, 1989), p. 99.
[27] Ibid.

respond to, you can't trust what you may think you perceive 'within' either.

The contrasts here may be too starkly drawn, too cavalier about the degree to which the speaker is inevitably deceived about the nature of his or her interiority (Augustine was already fascinated by the inaccessibility and alienness of speaking minds to themselves); and the sense in which 'being' is capable of being uttered, the contract or covenant of word and world, has regularly been fingered over by philosophers unconvinced about neat relations between words and external objects, without a resultant nihilism. Hegel, for instance, does not describe any *contract* between language and what it is not, but seeks to trace, how, in the processes of thinking and speaking, we are drawn (if we are willing to abide the necessary moments of frustration and contradiction) into an intelligent life whose perspective is neither limitedly or exclusively mine *nor* that of 'no one in particular', and which is truthful to the extent that it transcends the perspective of any one historical agent or moment. But it would certainly be true to say that Hegel assumes a massive act of trust or faith in the historical adventure of thought-in-community; and Steiner is right to see the turn of the late modern and postmodern world as radically and newly fragmentary.

Part of Hegel's insight, however, also has to do with the more overtly political matter of how in our dealings with one another we move towards a common life, a system of *Recht* (not quite 'law', not exactly 'right', but something close to 'public rationality' as it affects behaviour, not only discourse), which all recognise as embodying their true interest. Steiner at least compels us to attend to the erosion of trust at the basis of intellectual life; but what happens when this is complemented by the erosion of trust in corporate and political life? Ours is increasingly a situation in which ordinary citizens don't (and can't) take it for granted that the institutions of society can be relied upon to work in their interest. Education, healthcare, the law, are increasingly seen as bureaucratic and incompetent systems, consuming public funds in labyrinthine adminis-tration. Cynicism about government in general spills over into cynicism about public services; and the law is an obvious target for suspicion about whose interests are being served. These alienations – well-founded or not – are far more strongly marked in the USA than in Britain, and suspicion of central government has led to reactions of an increasingly feverish and paranoid character.

'Fightings within and fears without', as the hymn puts it: I am not recognisable to (thinking, speaking) self; I am not recognisable to a non-competitive other, not seen or attended to; I cannot recognise myself, my truth or interest or welfare, in the common life. The question that presses urgently through all this is what I can then say or do that is not in some sense violent. There are of course inescapable 'violences' in all speech and action. Gillian Rose wrote of the 'violence in love' and the 'love in violence',[28] both of which we seek to avoid in an unthinking fear of risk. Love stakes a position, and so cannot help risking the displacement or damaging of another. It is never far from violence. But violence itself seeks recognition, is a rebellion against solitary withdrawal

[28] Gillian Rose, *The Broken Middle. Out of Our Ancient Society* (Oxford, 1992), see esp. pp. 147–52.

and closure; and, in appealing to otherness in that way, is obliquely connected with love's search for life in the other. But when violence is taken out of this dialectical under-standing, when it becomes more and more clamant and insistent because its expectation of recognition is more and more eroded, the 'love in violence' is more and more securely imprisoned, frustrated in its residual urge towards converse. The loss of the soul becomes the loss of a *social*, not merely an individual, body.

'Where you are is where you are not,' wrote Eliot, paraphrasing St John of the Cross:[29] the recurring paradox is that our presence in the social body is only assured by the gift of a regard from outside, and that such regard is itself perceived and received only when we are dispossessed of a particular conception of presence. What has to come under judgement is the 'presence' of a single integrated system of needs and desires that is inherently violent and competitive. I become socially present when this is undermined in some degree, when the 'finished' self, justified to itself and in terms of itself, is absent; which means that to be socially present is to be present as a *soul* – as that which emerges through the disciplines of non-gratification or deferral, through love, through being seen. My presence in language, in converse and *intelligible* (that is, shared) action is grounded in an absence, the absence of the fantasy-fulfilment in which ego and object complement and 'finalise' each other (this is *for me*; I am satis-factorily myself *because of this*). And this absence is achieved in a complex set of dispossessions, sought and unsought – the 'defining conflicts' of Walter Davis's analysis, the moment when the subject discovers that its being is 'at issue'.

[29] T. S. Eliot, *Four Quartets* 'East Coker' (1940), pt. 3.

But what was said earlier should alert us to the risk here of a further turn of anxiety. Being 'where you are not', being dispossessed of the clear and well-defended site that the modern ego dreams of, may be understood simply as an absorption into an endless chain of displacement – the workings of the contingent other, the other who, in fact, mirrors my own contingency and instability. And because the contingent other is an other *like me*, the shadow of rivalry is never wholly absent. That is why this chapter has returned repeatedly to the language of the non-contingent other, the other that is *sufficiently* other not to compete with me for any imaginable space, logical, psychological, material, social: the 'non-existent Other', whose absence as just another agent or presence makes possible my own exodus from the imprisoning model of presence with which I'm likely to start. And here is the basic choice, call it metaphysical, religious or even just narrative. Is the absent Other that makes possible my own saving absence and social presence simply a construct, a linguistic device to spring me from my trap and no more? It is, of course, *at least* a linguistic construct, it appears in and only in the ways in which we speak to each other, socially and 'privately'; but can it be read without remainder as a tactic to enable the soul to emerge?

Say the answer to that is Yes; the implications are not promising. If it is in some sense *my* tactic, what I do to secure my release, it is a device of precisely that will which I must displace. It risks being a self-projection, built upon a fundamentally unchallenged ego. If it is the tactic of a contingent other, how can it avoid being seen as a tactic deployed by one ego to secure a desired effect in another? We have seen the delicacy of the disciplines needed in the analytic relationship if such misunderstanding is to be checked; but on what do such disciplines rest, on what curious faith in the *validity* or legitimacy of talking like this in the first place about an identity shaped by the evoking of a significant absence? Is it ultimately the case that language is the engagement of contingent others with each other, however it may seek to limit the damage done, by means of oblique evocations of something else? Postmodernist theory itself gestures characteristically towards a non-presence that we can't help indicating – the marginal, the region of *différance*, that which surrounds speech because it is what speech both does not say and 'says' by refusing it. But in what sense this could be an Other that made anything possible is obscure: if anything, it tends to reduce the idea of social presence itself to an abstraction. The speaker is the site on which forces converge and contend: *I* am absent, not as yielding place or recognising myself in the other, but because I am the gratuitous and impotent deposit of the freezing or solidifying of one moment or aspect of the contest of forces.

The question nagging away behind all this is whether it makes sense to imagine the absent Other as somehow analogous to the giver of a gift. Hence – again – the drift in these concluding reflections towards a religious construction of the absent Other. Buddhism, which has invested so much, with such sophistication, in the language of absence, not-self and so on, insists that any actual imagining of the sheer 'that' which makes us free and lies beyond desire and self-representation will return us ultimately to the bondage of desire. It is an important and serious challenge to the insistence of the eastern Mediterranean religious traditions that, whatever the risk we have no choice but to speak at *some* point about gift or love, and therefore to recognise in the Other something like intelligence and action. Better the admitted paradox of a self-dispossessing divinity, say these traditions, better the puzzling evocations of an agency that is unqualified gift or 'bestowal' than the risk of the unqualified abstractness of the Buddhist discourse, the pointing to a wholly indeterminate There or That.

Needless to say, there is no objective way of settling the issue between these two (or any other set of) traditions. Both involve different but not unrelated forms of the disciplines of a controlled frustration of desire; both give considerable importance to *corporate* ritual practice as the context for the re-formation of the self. But what I have called the eastern Mediterranean (Jewish, Christian and Muslim) discourses all give a pivotal place in their language to *gratitude* – the acknowledgement that I am acted *on* before I act or can act. The absent other in language is there-and-not-there because we are always already spoken *to*. This is expressed formally in the concept of a creation from nothing – a doctrine that establishes very plainly why the divine is not *an* other, within a system of interlocking or negotiating agencies; and why – to refer back to one of the oldest axioms in the Mediterranean religious tradition – there is no 'envy' in the divine. There is by definition nothing to compete for, so that it actually becomes possible to imagine the divine as the source of unqualified gift.

The Christian tradition in particular elaborates a bit further, in the proposals that God is, intrinsically and independently of the universe, a 'system' or pattern of agency and relation (trinity), and that God's agency is present without qualification within the material identity of one historical agent (Jesus Christ). The first of these prohibits the Christian from conceiving the otherness of the divine as in *any* way like that of one other subject in a system. The second reinforces and deepens the prohibition against seeing the divine and what is other to it as in *any* way competing for the same space (since God and the human are 'located' in exactly the same place in this particular person). Much more would need to be said about how these religious conceptualities relate to what has been addressed in this book; my point here is only to indicate how they might be read as attempts to construct, in the light of a complex historical narrative of divine action, a resourceful language for the 'non-existent Other' which is at the foundations of speech and sociality.

Perhaps predictably, in the light of all this, the Christian tradition both represents these doctrinal notions *and* refuses to settle for any representation as exhaustive. In the early centuries of the Christian Church, there were heated debates over the correct or adequate way of articulating belief, debates that have been the object of polite wonder and not-so-polite mockery from Gibbon to the present day. Alongside these debates, however, ran a complementary development, the refining of a theology of 'denial' or 'unsaying', *apophasis*: by all means struggle to get the least misleading formula, because words do matter, and how you represent God affects what you are going to find possible for yourself and for the human community; but equally, don't mistake the words for a description of what it is like to be God, of the 'essence' of the divine. These words are not labels (strictly speaking, no words are simply labels anyway) but something more like codes of instruction, directions as to how to shape and discipline your seeing and your reacting to what's given.

And it is out of this particular balancing act that the Christian icon emerges in its full theological sense. By the eighth century of the Common Era, and in the teeth of some savage religio-political struggles, Eastern Christianity had elaborated a theory and practice of *pictorial* representation corresponding to its theory and practice of *verbal* representation. The Byzantine icon is not meant to reproduce a set of empirical data – how Christ or the saints happened to look, what heaven is supposed to be like. The famous fourteenth-century depiction of the Trinity by Andrei Rublev, the extraordinary frescoes of his teacher Feofan, the works of the 'Palaeologue Renaissance' in Constantinople with their athletic figures throwing off light as if soaked in some phosphorescent liquid – these are not an attempt to show you what God or the things of heaven look like. The Church that commissioned and used such images knew perfectly well that God and heaven – and even, in an important sense, the events of a holy life – don't 'look like' anything, and that the divine reality can't be rendered exhaustively in material terms. The image gives directions, it essays a way of bringing you into a new place and a new perception.

It does at least two preliminary things – and one central thing of some importance for the argument of this book. It shows bodily realities – the face of Christ or Mary, the portraits of saints, episodes from biblical or hagiological story – as suffused with divine action: the bodies are stylised and configured into patterns, often patterns of violent energy and often underlined by an apparently anarchic but in fact tightly worked scattering of highlights.

There are no light sources outside the frame: light, pattern, significance, move *out* from a base or centre. Second, and in consequence of this, the eye is invited, or instructed, to move repeatedly *in* to this base or centre, to the sources of light. But it has many times been stressed that the *perspective* of iconic representation totally refuses anything like the convergent point of disappearance familiar in Western representational art. The 'centre' is not a distant abstract point but something at work *in* the luminous surface itself. In many instances, perspective is apparently reversed: the convergent point is the eye itself, as if the painted surface were a window into another geometrical order.[30]

But the most important feature here is what both these highly self-conscious grotesqueries are attempting to encode. The person looking at the icon is invited (instructed?) to let go of being an agent observing a motionless phenomenon: the idiom of the painting insists on its own activity, its 'bearing down' upon the beholder, shedding rather than receiving light, gathering and directing its energy rather than spreading from an invisible point of convergence. And this finds its fullest expression in the iconographer's depiction of the eyes of Christ or the saints (no saint is ever shown in profile). As the perspective 'bears down' upon the beholder's eye, the eye of the iconic figure acts, searches, engages. The skill of looking at icons, the discipline of 'reading' them, is indeed the strange skill of letting yourself be seen, be read.

The religious icon is an evocation of the non-existent

[30] On inverse perspective in icons, see, for example, Leonid Ouspensky, 'The Meaning and Language of Icons' in Leonid Ouspensky and Vladimir Lossky, *The Meaning of Icons* (2nd ed. Crestwood, NY, 1982), pp. 25–49, p. 41.

Other simply by its subversion of what we might expect in a devotional artefact. It does not work to stimulate emotion or clarify ideas or add concreteness to a process of reflection: it requires first that I take time to follow (obey) those surface movements that indicate the inner centre of illumination; then that I stand to *be* illuminated, to be the object of whatever is at work. The non-existent Other is here the absence of any imaginable or conceivable reality 'behind' the icon's surface, some further level capable of inspection: there is no normal perspectival hinterland. Or you could say that its otherness is in the fact that the icon is always a wall that confronts (at the same time as being a rather peculiar kind of window), that can't be seen from the back, and so does not occupy a space *alongside* me, does not share the dimension I inhabit. But so much of this in fact returns to the theme of the icon as what I am seen *by*: the eyes with which I must engage but cannot negotiate – because they do not hold a position like mine – occupy a dimensional point of view.

The 'lost icons' of this book have been clusters of convention and imagination, images of possible lives or modes of life, possible positions to occupy in a world that is inexorably one of time and loss. But as the discussion has developed, it has hinted more and more at a single, focal area of lost imagination – what I have called the lost soul. And *this* loss, I've suggested, is inextricably linked with the loss of what is encoded in the actual icons of Christian tradition and usage – the Other who does not compete, with whom I don't have to and can't bargain; the Other beyond violence, the regard that will not be evaded or deflected, yet has and seeks no advantage. What has been culturally lost, the sense of being educated into adult

186

choice, the possibility (tantalisingly both political and more than political) of social miracle, active appropriation of a common good, the possibility of letting go of a possessed and defended image of the moral self, abstractly free, self-nurturing – all this will remain lost without a recovered confidence in the therapeutic Other, not 'there' for examination, for contest, even for simple consolation; so hard to say anything about without risking the corruption of the consolatory voice. But sometimes, whatever the risk, we have to force ourselves to talk, not of consolation but of hope, of what is not or cannot be lost. We *can* choose death, but we don't have to. What we are present to is neither created nor extinguished by our will. The iconic eye remains wakeful.

Index